Interest Groups and
Monetary Integration

The Political Economy of Global Interdependence

Thomas Willett, Series Editor

Interest Groups and Monetary Integration

The Political Economy of Exchange Regime Choice

Carsten Hefeker

WestviewPress

A Division of HarperCollins*Publishers*

The Political Economy of Global Interdependence

Copyright © 1997 by Westview Press, A Division of HarperCollins Publishers, Inc.

Published in 1997 in the United States of America by Westview Press, 5500 Central Avenue, Boulder,
Colorado 80301-2877, and in the United Kingdom by Westview Press, 12 Hid's Copse Road,
Cumnor Hill, Oxford OX2 9JJ

A CIP catalog record for this book is available from the Library of Congress.
ISBN 0-8133-3278-8 (hc)

The paper used in this publication meets the requirements of the American National Standard for
Permanence of Paper for Printed Library Materials Z39.48-1984.

10   9   8   7   6   5   4   3   2   1

Contents

1

Introduction

The currency question, Disreali is reported to have said, has made even more persons mad than love. A quantitative test of the accuracy of this comparison is, in the present deplorable state of medical statistics, scarcely possible. But Disraeli may well have been right.

-Jacob Viner, 1932

Currency crises at the periphery of Europe, the common currency project for Europe, and the ongoing problems of the economies in transition in Eastern Europe and the former Soviet Union suggest that the currency question is still far from being solved. In 1992 a series of speculative crises started which brought down the European Exchange Rate System as it had existed. Italy and Great Britain were forced to abandon the European Monetary System (EMS) altogether, and several other currencies were forced to devalue while the system as a whole moved to wider bands.[1] Nevertheless, European governments have expressed their determination to reach European Monetary Union by the end of this century. At the same time, it is not clear that the exchange rate regime choices the reforming economies in Central and Eastern Europe have made will prove to be adequate and stable, while countries in South America and Asia face the threat of currency crises.

What is striking for the observer is that the advice economists have to offer on the choice of the exchange rate regime is so often disregarded. If one examines the evolution of the international monetary system in the last hundred years or so, one observes a pattern common to many nations and to most of the European countries. Periods of fixed exchange rate regimes are followed by periods of floating rates. And after a more or less prolonged period of flexible exchange rates, there is a general tendency to return to some sort of fixed exchange rate regime, regardless of what economists identify as the adequate regime.[2]

Beginning in the mid-nineteenth century in the course of nation-building, formerly independent states moved towards the adoption of a national currency, sometimes even accompanied by attempts to form monetary unions across national borders. Likewise, the common gold standard of the 1880s was the adoption of a fixed exchange rate *vis-à-vis* a common monetary basis that broke down with World War I. The interwar years saw a rapid sequence of different exchange rate regimes: from 1921 to 1926 freely floating rates, from 1927 through 1931 fixed rates, and managed floating for the rest of the 1930s. These regimes were followed after the second world war by the Bretton Woods system of adjustable fixed exchange rates. After its formal dissolution in 1973, European economies made attempts to fix their exchange rates among themselves. First the "snake", a fixed exchange rate system, was launched, and in 1979 the European Monetary System followed. The latter, in turn, is itself characterized by phases of enthusiasm for full monetary union, expressed in the Werner and Delors Reports and the Maastricht Treaty, and phases when that idea was relegated to the future. This evidence suggests that monetary authorities have a preference for fixing the exchange rate and do so unless prevented by particularly adverse circumstances. Are there thus predictable cycles in exchange rate regimes and what underlies them?

That is the question this study seeks to answer. Although there exist some empirical studies that try to assess the performance of different regimes in terms of output stabilization and price stability, they often take the choice of the regime as given (Alogoskoufis and Smith 1991; Baxter and Stockman 1989; Bayoumi and Eichengreen 1994). The studies which focus on the choice of exchange rate regimes have their problems as well. They are mostly concerned with developing countries (Savvides 1990), which have only restricted comparability to European economies, or are unable to find evidence that is consistent with their own theoretical expectations (Honkapohja and Pikkarainnen 1994). Moreover, they all work with the (implicit) assumption of a welfare maximizing government. What the theoretical literature in contrast has to offer is either concerned with the normative choice of an exchange rate regime, the recently revived optimum currency area debate. Or it analyzes the collapse of fixed exchange rate regimes, but without being able to convincingly derive the reason for the choice of the regime in the first place.

This is why I develop an alternative approach which attempts to give a better explanation of what we observe. I combine the choice and the collapse of fixed exchange rates and monetary integration in an endogenous political-economic approach. The choice of an exchange rate regime is political in the sense that the decision to adopt this regime is not made by a benevolent social planner weighing the costs and benefits for the nation. Rather is it the outcome of a political process where voters and interest groups interact, which support or oppose the initiative depending on how it is likely to affect their individual welfare, not the welfare of the nation as a whole. What is important in this approach is that it combines domestic politics with the history and presence of the international monetary system. I argue that international economic policy can only be adequately understood by taking domestic politics explicitly into account.

Efforts in the same direction have already been made by several other authors. Eichengreen and Frieden (1993) for example argue that traders might prefer fixed exchange rates, and Vaubel (1991) and Havrilevsky (1994) study the behavior of central banks. But to my knowledge, no other study has yet brought all this literature together, nor has any other study developed a coherent framework where all these arguments find their place. This study should therefore be seen as a contribution to a field where more work is needed.

Some of the results I arrive at are empirically compatible with the predictions of optimum currency area (see Al-Marhubi and Willett 1995) although they derive from a different approach. That evidence is thus consistent with different theoretical approaches and not a proof for the optimum currency area theory. And as I argue in Chapter 2, I do not regard the theoretical basis for optimum currency area theory as convincing.

1.1. The Argument of the Book

Two themes run through this book. The first, and usually neglected one, is that international monetary relations are closely connected with the trading system. In international economics, however, discussions of the international monetary system and the international trading system are usually separated. Links are implied but rarely elucidated. The main point I make is that the emergence of a stable and smoothly functioning international monetary system is driven by and hinges on international trade.

The gold standard was stable at its European core because it was built on a multilateral trading system with important complementarities between financial and commodity markets. The stability of the Bretton Woods system similarly was based on the expanding multilateral trading system. In both periods, the stability of the international monetary system had a positive feedback on the stability of the trading system. Given this symbiosis, serious shocks to either the trading system or the monetary system could bring both tumbling down (Eichengreen 1995).[3] Thus, I argue in this book that monetary integration is basically driven by the underlying trade integration and follows it. The impetus for monetary integration is reduced when trade collapses, as Chapters 3 and 7 will show.

The connection between domestic politics and international economics is the second theme of this book. Politics enters at two levels. First, domestic political pressures influence governments' choice of international economic policies.

Second, domestic political pressures influence the credibility of governments' commitments to policies and hence their economic effects. The credibility of the gold standard derived from the priority attached by governments to the maintenance of balance of payments equilibrium. There was little doubt in the core countries that the authorities would go a long way to defend the central banks' gold reserves. If one of the banks lost reserves and its exchange rates weakened, funds would flow in from abroad in anticipation of the capital gains investors would reap once authorities adopted measures to stem the reserve losses and strengthen the exchange rate. Since there was no question about the commitment, capital would flow in considerable amounts to stabilize the exchange rate. Thus capital flows were stabilizing and the commitment to gold was rarely tested by speculators.

That credibility was closely connected to international cooperation. When stabilizing speculation and domestic intervention proved incapable of accommodating a disturbance, the system was stabilized through cooperation among governments and central banks. In major crises, when interest rate reactions were not sufficient, lending of gold funds among central banks was forthcoming, and hence the gold reserves a central bank could use to defend its parity was far greater than its own reserves. With the first world war and the changes in the political systems this all changed as well (Eichengreen 1995).[4] As Triffin (1947: 57) observed, "The most significant development of the period was the growing importance of domestic factors as the final determinant of monetary policies." Thus, when domestic political pressures become important for economic policy, international commitments and cooperation are subordinated to those domestic aims. International economic relations and stability are ultimately a function of and dependent on domestic politics.[5]

1.2. The Structure of the Book

In Chapter 2, I review the literature on the choice and collapse of exchange rate regimes and point out its flaws. The optimum currency area literature is insufficient because it is not able to explain fully the observed choice of exchange rate regimes. Likewise, the interpretation of fixed exchange rates as a monetary policy rule is unconvincing for theoretical and practical reasons. The literature on the collapse of exchange rate regimes in contrast lacks a convincing explanation for the choice of fixed rates in the first place. This chapter argues that both, choice and collapse, need to be combined in one model. Consequently, I develop an alternative endogenous political economy approach to analyze the choice and collapse of exchange rate regimes. In particular, the interest group approach is introduced and a basic model is developed on which the following chapters build.

Chapter 3 begins with a historical overview of monetary integration in nine-teenth-century Europe, which is the geographic center of this book. The nine-teenth century was chosen as a starting point because industrial interests increasingly began to play a decisive role in shaping politics, whereas in earlier times monetary integration mainly followed hegemonic extension.

A natural differentiation is made between monetary integration in the course of nation building--the cases of Germany, Switzerland and Italy--and attempts of supranational integration--the cases of the Austro-German Monetary Union, the Latin Monetary Union and the Scandinavian Monetary Union. In contrast to recent work on this subject (Bergman et al. 1993; Flandreau 1993a; Redish 1993a; Theurl 1992), the focus is on the influence of interest groups and how they influenced the processes observed. Basically the chapter finds that industrial interests in monetary integration were mainly driven by trade integration. There is, hence, a close connection with the well-known cycles in trade integration and recurrent protectionism in the nineteenth century (Irwin 1993; Mc Keown 1983). Increasing trade in the middle of the nineteenth century was underlying growing industrial pressures for common currency standards between trading regions. These industrial interests found initially support in hegemonic political interests (especially Prussia and France) which saw monetary integration as one way to establish also political dominance over other states. Hence industry and politicians formed a coalition. An opposing coalition was built between the gainers from seigniorage, that is banks of emission and the fiscal authorities of these states. Over time this coalition could be overcome and compensated by fiscal redistribution at the national level and by granting temporarily the rights to issue paper money. In the national cases the free-rider problem among issuing authorities could be solved by establishing a common central bank.

The supranational cases, however, could not find such a constitutional solu-tion. They were moreover characterized by abiding interests in free trade as the European recession after 1870 led to increased protectionist pressures. The pro-integration coalition was further weakened by the hegemonic decline of the once dominant powers. External shocks, especially wars, and the thus increased fiscal needs of governments rendered cooperative behavior even more difficult as these were largely covered through money creation. A final reason is that a compensation mechanism for the losers from monetary integration was not present in the supranational cases.

Chapter 4 develops a two-country model to explain the endogenous choice of exchange rate regimes. A political support maximizing government balances interests for and against exchange rate stability and determines thus the policy decisions to be taken. The conflict in the economy is given between the tradable and the non-tradable goods producing sectors where the former wishes to adopt fixed exchange rates while the latter wants to retain monetary autonomy. When external shocks occur, the government's decision may be revised because the importance of stabilization policy increases. In the two country setting chosen, it becomes clear how these domestic influences shape and determine the international economic policy of a government. The exchange rate peg will be given up by one country as soon as domestic policy aims are no longer compatible with the peg. As argued by optimum currency area theory, asymmetric shocks can break up such a fixed rate arrangement. In the second part of that chapter the reasons for monetary union are derived by highlighting the role of capital mobility. This part is the foundation for the next chapters which focus on European monetary integration since it derives the reason why European countries have decided to move from the European Monetary System towards full monetary union.

Chapter 5, the first chapter focusing exclusively on European Monetary Union (EMU), discusses the industrial interests in monetary union. The discussion of those interests is centered on the financial industry. This for two reasons: First, part of that industry is very outspoken in its desire to have monetary union, much more than any other industry. And second, in that industry a conflict between small and large enterprises is most visible and makes it possible to derive distributional conflicts *within* the tradables industry. The chapter is therefore a qualification to the monolithic picture painted of the tradables industry in Chapter 4. The basic point developed is that large commercial banks hope to gain market share in transborder financial services to the costs of the smaller banks. First, the necessary unification of banking directives and regulation by a single central bank makes transborder financial business cheaper for all international banks. Secondly, because of economies-of-scale, larger banks are more able to cooperate internationally. This enables them to supply cross-border financial services cheaper and thus to gain a larger market share.

Chapter 6, the second chapter on EMU, turns to bureaucratic interests, as exemplified by central banks. While the hypothesis derived in the literature is that central banks favor monetary union, this statement has to be qualified for the German central bank, the Bundesbank. It is obvious, and has been noted before, that the German central bank is the bank which has most to lose from monetary union because it loses its dominant position in Europe. This is highlighted by analyzing one particular and important phase in the history of the European Monetary System, namely the collapse of the EMS in 1993. I suggest that the Bundesbank used the idiosyncratic shock of German unification and the following monetary expansion as a justification for extremely tight monetary policy. With this it embarked on a course of undermining the other EMS countries' support for EMU. The tight monetary policy had, of course, spill-over effects onto the EMS partner countries. Those had to raise their interest rates to defend the exchange rates against the rising deutsche mark. With the upcoming recession in Europe, these countries were no longer able to resist devaluationary pressures by further increasing interest rates. Domestic political pressure resulted in a relaxing of the exchange rate constraint. More precisely, markets' perceptions of these political pressures and their resulting speculation caused a breakdown of the EMS (Portes 1993). Thus, this chapter suggests that the idiosyncratic real shock of German unification and the Bundesbank's reluctance to monetary union in Europe were responsible for the EMS collapse.

Chapter 7 closes the circle in drawing a close connection between the motives for the collapse of monetary integration in the nineteenth century and the similar reasons behind the collapse of the common ruble zone in the former Soviet Union. In this case, as before, political motives and nationalism have a distinct political influence and are more important than in the case of the European Union.[6] Moreover, seigniorage revenue has an important role in the financing of the budget of governments and this gives again rise to free-rider behavior of the countries in the ruble zone. This uncooperative behavior and the response to it are basically behind the collapse of the ruble zone. The chapter discusses in detail the distributional conflict behind this competitive money creation and asks whether and when industrial interests that favor stable exchange rates can bring the political process to move towards some form of monetary reintegration.

Chapter 8 briefly recapitulates the major arguments made in the preceding chapters and offers a personal view on the desirability of monetary integration.

This study has been prepared as a dissertation during my affiliation with the University of Konstanz. It has been financially supported by the Deutsche Forschungsgemeinschaft via the SFB 178 program. The Centre for European Policy Studies in Brussels provided a hospitable environment for revision. I thank all those institutions.

I am grateful to Rolf Bommer, Jeff Frieden, Daniel Gros, Arye Hillman, Carl-Ludwig Holtfrerich, Achim Körber, Mathias Moersch, Günther Schulze, and Roland Vaubel who commented on parts of this study. A visit to the Lowe Institute at Claremont McKenna College and discussions with Sven Arndt were most fruitful. I am especially indebted to series editor Tom Willett who read the whole manuscript and made invaluable comments and suggestions to improve it; to Hans Peter Grüner for discussions and collaboration; and to my advisers Heinrich W. Ursprung for support and encouragement and Nikolaus K. A. Läufer for very helpful comments.

Notes

1. The bands in which currencies may move have been widened from generally ± 2.5 percent to generally ± 15 percent around the central parity.

2. Throughout the study, I use fixed and pegged exchange rates interchangeably since I am mainly concerned with the regime choice and not with in-between arrangements like crawling pegs. I do not think that irrevocably fixed exchange rates exist, except in a full monetary union. Permanently fixed exchange rates is an "oxymoron", because exchange rates exist to be changed (Portes 1993). Thus, the differentiation between fixed and pegged exchange rates is an artificial one.

3. The relations between trade and the monetary system are discussed in Simmons (1994) for the interwar period.

4. As Temin (1989) shows, there were ill fated attempts at restoring the gold standard after World War I and only after the great depression realized countries that a change in the regime away from the gold standard was needed. The shift of focus towards full employment resulted in the "mixed economy" of the post-World War II era.

5. James (1995) shows how the Bretton Woods system aimed at combining international stability without surrendering domestic policy autonomy since the dominance of international stability was thought to have caused the troubles of the interwar period. See also Giovannini (1993a) for a debate of the different positions taken by the British and the U.S. government in this discussion.

6. To be sure, I do not argue that these aspects are unimportant in the EU case. I only state that nationalism is more important in the former Soviet Union than in the European Union.

2

The Economics and the Politics
of Exchange Rate Regimes

This chapter begins with a review of the literature on the choice of exchange rate regimes. The problem has been formalized by the so-called optimum currency area theory; and more recently the choice of fixed exchange rates has been interpreted as a monetary rule. I discuss the two approaches and offer an alternative interpretation by introducing politically self-interested governments.[1] Since politics has been introduced in monetary affairs by the political business cycle literature, I briefly discuss the approach as well, as it has been extended to exchange rates recently. It comes closest to my own arguments, but without introducing interest groups explicitly. I then apply the interest group model to the collapse of fixed exchange rates and discuss subsequently two important changes during the time horizon of this study. First, the democratization of society has changed the political constraints governments face in economic policy. In contrast to the last century, with which this study deals in Chapter 3, monetary policy in this century has increasingly become politicized, with important implications for the exchange rate choice as well. Secondly, capital controls, working for most of the time in this century loosened the constraints of monetary policy. The abolishment of capital controls as part of the single market program in Europe, however, has put another constraint on monetary and exchange rate policy.

2.1. Monetary Integration in the Literature

Before discussing the literature on the choice of exchange rate regimes, two general remarks on the issue of monetary integration seem are in order. First, there is no generally accepted definition in the literature as to what monetary integration means. As there are various degrees of integration on the real side of international economics (ranging from free-trade areas to a common market), there are as well various degrees of integration on the monetary side. Tavlas (1993) distinguishes four degrees of monetary integration: (i) exchange rate unions, where the parities between the participants are irrevocably fixed but monetary policies need not be coordinated, (ii) pseudo exchange rate unions that involve fixed rates among the members and free capital mobility, but without having a formal integration of monetary policies, (iii) monetary integration, which is used interchangeably with currency areas, has also irrevocably fixed exchange rates without any margin of fluctuation, but additionally includes full capital mobility, financial market integration and a common monetary policy, and (iv) full monetary union which adds a single currency and a common central bank. Chapter 3 will deal with the classification (ii), but it will also become clear why this is an unstable arrangement. The discussion will then move on to arrangements comparable to (iii) and (iv).

The second general problem is that economic theory is still unable to provide a sound theoretical or empirical estimate concerning the costs and benefits of a common money (see also Eichengreen and Ghironi 1995; Viñals 1996).[2] The reason is that money remains a difficult variable for economists to model. Only recently some progress on that question has been made. Drawing on the literature on network externalities, Kiyotaki and Wright (1989) show the advantages of money in general and Matsuyama et al. (1993) have shown how the efficiency advantages of a common currency can be modeled. These works, although promising, have the problem that they are hard to quantify empirically.

The problem directly extends to measuring the gains from stable exchange rates. While many people believe intuitively that exchange rate uncertainty reduces international trade, especially over the long horizon, attempts to estimate these effects depend on the assumptions of the structure of exchange rate risk. If one recognizes that trade effects exchange rate variability as well, and that different kinds of trade are likely to display different degrees of sensitivity to exchange rate variability, the difficulty to isolate the effects of exchange rate uncertainty econometrically is evident.

The same is true for the stabilization side of the exchange rate instrument. Giving up the exchange rate instrument hinges on the costs of doing so. Some macroeconomists believe that monetary policy is ineffectual for countering recessions because workers learn quickly to anticipate the inflationary effects of monetary expansion and adapt their wage demands accordingly. If, however, expansionary monetary policy only increases inflation then there is no cost in giving it up. Moreover, even if national monetary policy can be effective, it will be unnecessary if there exist other instruments of adjustment or if the incidence of disturbances is similar across countries. Again, the evidence is mixed on this point and only retrospective.[3] The structure of shocks under EMU is hard to imagine beforehand. Thus the effects from monetary unification are not easy to assess and economists can say little with confidence about the economic costs and benefits from monetary unification. This is one more reason to adopt a positive endogenous political perspective on this problem. Before doing so, I turn to the "traditional" literature on the costs and benefits of fixed exchange rates.

The Early Optimum Currency Area Literature

The literature on the desirability of monetary integration started in the sixties with the seminal analysis by Mundell (1961). He posed the problem of the optimum domain of one money for the first time.[4] It seemed to be clear that money is a convenience and that thus the optimum number of currencies should be restricted because the functions of money are better served the smaller the number of currencies in use.[5] From this alone, the optimum currency area would be the world. On the other hand, flexible rates and different moneys have advantages as well.

The argument for flexible parities runs as follows. Consider an asymmetric shock, for example a shift in demand from domestic to foreign products, requiring an adjustment in domestic costs to restore prices and demand to levels consistent with full employment. That is, a reduction in real wages is needed to price workers back into employment. If real wages are flexible, labor markets will complete the necessary adjustments without policy interventions. If nominal wages, however, are downwardly rigid, the theory maintains that a reduction in real wages can also be achieved by a devaluation of the exchange rate. Raising the price level by depreciating the home currency may achieve the real wage adjustment. The usefulness of flexible exchange rates, hence, is seen in its function as an adjustment mechanism, based on the assumption of rigid nominal wages. The assumption of downwardly rigid wages and money illusion was explicitly made by Mundell for he "assumed that the unions bargain for a money rather than a real wage, and adjust their wage demands to changes in the cost of living, if at all, only if the cost of living index excludes imports" (1961, 663).[6]

Thus, Mundell assumed that money wages and prices cannot be reduced in the short-run if there was a shift in demand between regions which required relative real incomes to change. Adjusting the exchange rate could thereby avoid the temporary costs of unemployment in one region and inflation in the other by bringing about the relative price shift between country through parity changes.[7]

The instrument of adjustment discussed by Mundell to substitute for exchange rate flexibility was the degree of factor mobility. If factors of production (usually discussed in terms of labor) move across industries (or across regions) the relative adjustment of wages takes place via this mechanism. For many years this has been the major lesson taken form the Mundell analysis, but it is probably the wage setting behavior across regions and industries that should be focused upon. The simple fact is that labor mobility will almost always be too low to justify a common currency because even labor mobility within countries and sometimes even within regions is certainly too low to play this role of adjustment. The major conclusion is thus that wages must be flexible downwards and that wage fixing must be enterprise and region specific. Reliance cannot be placed on labor mobility (Corden 1993).

This would imply that shocks have to be asymmetric across regions to make flexible exchange rates useful. And it suggests that monetary areas should be smaller than the national borders of today. For asymmetric shocks are likely to affect regions that are certainly smaller than countries like Germany or France. On the other hand, a particular money for any region or industry makes the usefulness of money smaller and smaller. Moreover, the underlying assumption of money illusion, giving rise to the real wage reducing role of exchange rate devaluation, loses its plausibility in extremely small regions.

This point was made by Mc Kinnon who continued the optimum currency area debate in 1963 with a natural extension of Mundell's arguments. He focused on the maintenance of a stable price level in a currency area. The greater the ratio of tradable to non-tradable goods, the less stable will the price level be in a flexible rate regime (under the price-taker assumption). The assumption was that monetary policy kept the prices on non-tradables stable and that tradables prices fluctuated because of real shocks rather than because of foreign inflation. The summary is that the smaller a country is, the less appropriate would be a flexible exchange rate.

Kenen (1969) finally introduced a third optimum currency area concept. The more diverse the product mix of a country is, and especially the more diverse its exports, the less it is likely to suffer from generalized adverse shocks and thus the less it is likely to need exchange rate adjustments. This would imply that two large well-diversified countries like France and Germany could form an optimum currency area. As Tower and Willett (1976) noted, the criteria do oppose because in the Mundell-Mc Kinnon stories the smaller the country the less it is likely to be an optimum currency area. But according to Kenen it might be exactly a country's small size which makes it an optimum currency area because its production is probably not diversified enough for fixed exchange rates.

Finally, in the seventies, the Phillips-Curve was introduced to determine an optimum currency area. Corden (1972) argued that countries had different Phillips curves for a variety of reasons, including labor unions' wage aggressiveness, and differed in their social preferences between unemployment and inflation. Magnifico (1973) even introduced the concept of "national propensities to inflation". If those differ, countries should not form a currency union.

The critique to these considerations is that they hinge on the assumption of money and exchange rate illusion. But as Mc Kinnon (1963), in his contribution to the optimum currency area discussion noted, in a country with a large share of tradables in GDP, a nominal depreciation would have strong effects on the domestic price level and workers would immediately realize the deterioration in their standard of living and require compensation. The conclusion is that highly open economies are probably not characterized by wage illusion of workers.[8]

Secondly, and more serious, a change in the *general* price level is inappropriate to help *specific* industries to adjust to exogenous shocks. It, in contrast, might even result in distortions in other sectors than the one originally affected (Hayek 1937). This is because devaluation means that all domestic prices fall *vis-à-vis* foreign prices to restore international equilibrium instead of lowering the relative price of the home good immediately affected. Thus, the derivation of the benefit of flexible exchange rates for a country is implicitly based on a one-good economy model. This is obviously an inappropriate and useless model in this context. Countries with diversified production structures, like the European economies, raise doubts about the appropriateness of exchange rate changes as an adjustment device. The exchange rate is the wrong instrument because it can only shift the whole price level of one country *vis-à-vis* the other countries. While leading to the desired change in relative prices, it also changes all other relative price relations between domestic and foreign goods (Hefeker 1995a).

Hence the adjustment function of exchange rates is only given for country-specific shocks that become increasingly unlikely to occur in Europe. Similar production structures and more intra-industry trade subject countries to similar shocks. Only for shocks which hit a whole nation asymmetrically in form of monetary supply shocks, or of nation-specific shocks to the velocity of circulation, to the stability of the banking system, to the level of wages or to the productivity of labor, are exchange rate changes an appropriate instrument for international adjustments. Given that European countries seem to develop similar inflation preferences (Collins and Giavazzi 1993),[9] making asymmetric monetary policy shocks less likely, this instrument may no longer be needed. And, by definition, asymmetric money supply shocks can no longer occur in a monetary union.

Recent Approaches

In the eighties the Keynesian framework has been discredited by the introduction of rational-expectations into macroeconomics and substituted by the discussion about time-inconsistency and rules versus discretion in monetary policy. In this framework the question is whether fixed exchange rate raise the credibility of monetary policy. The literature has answered this question in the affirmative.

According to this argument, the exchange rate question is just part of a general discussion about rules versus discretion in monetary policy (Kydland and Prescott 1977; Barro and Gordon 1983). That discussion is based on the fact that policymakers, being aware of temporal rigidities in the labor market, such as fixed-period wage contracts, are tempted to inflate prices in order to lower the real wages paid under those contracts. This would induce firms to hire more labor, because the real price of labor is reduced, expanding employment and output. If, however, workers as rational individuals understand this incentive for the policymaker they incorporate an inflationary mark-up into their nominal wage demands to ensure a constant real wage. Therefore, the economy ends up with higher inflation and no output effects. Even worse, if inflation is expected by the population, the central bank has to fulfill this expectation because it would otherwise cause employment and output to fall. Promises of policymakers and central bankers not to inflate are not credible because, once contracts have been written, they are tempted to renege on their promises and to surprise wage-setters with inflation. This happens although governments do oppose inflation as well. As long as the marginal benefits from employment gains are larger than the costs in terms of higher inflation, governments will try to achieve inflationary surprises. Therefore, for non-inflationary announcements to be credible, monetary policy rules are required which prevent time-inconsistent policies. Exchange rates are seen as one such binding commitment.

Fixed exchange rates not only constrain surprises in money growth but also exclude the same time-inconsistent behavior in direct exchange rate manipulation (see Edwards 1993). Governments that have the possibility to alter the exchange rate will tend to abuse their power, introducing an inflationary bias into the economy. By an unexpected devaluation the government expects to induce a reduction of real wages and to increase output and employment. Again, the rational public recognizes the government's incentive, anticipates the devaluation and makes it hence ineffective. Particularly the EMS has been interpreted as such an external commitment by European countries. By pegging their currencies to the relatively stable deutsche mark, they "tied their hands" (Giavazzi and Pagano 1988) and imported credibility of their monetary policy (Melitz 1988).

The latest, but related, theme that arose in this literature focused on the optimal rate of inflation in a public-finance approach. This approach views inflation as a form of revenue (seigniorage) and considers thus monetary policy as part of a more global government budget problem. This is a different but not necessarily alternative theory to the Barro-Gordon story to explain inflation. Faced with an exogenous expenditure stream to be financed, the government chooses the optimal mix of taxes and debt. In general, seigniorage will be part of an efficient revenue policy (Grilli 1989). Optimum currency areas are thus derived along the lines of seigniorage needs of countries (see Canzoneri and Rogers 1990).

This approach has recently been extended to the decision of governments to temporarily suspend the fixed exchange rate regime to be able to collect higher seigniorage revenues, thereby endogenizing exchange rate regime switches. De Kock and Grilli (1993) analyze a model where the real interest rate is uncertain because of stochastic inflationary policy motivated by revenue requirements. Agents, however, have the opportunity to invest in costly information gathering activities to better forecast the inflation rate and can then trade on asset markets to profit from their informational advantage. But this situation implies losses for the economy which could be avoided by fixing exchange rates and reducing uncertainty. The authorities on the other hand face the trade-off between fixed exchange rates and revenue collection. During periods of relatively moderate levels of expenditures and low revenue requirement, it would be optimal to fix the exchange rate in order to avoid the aforementioned losses. On the other hand, sudden increases in the level of expenditure, or increases in the costs of using alternative tax instruments may make it preferable to incur these welfare losses in return for seigniorage revenues. Once the value of using seigniorage revenues decreases again, monetary authorities will find it optimal to revert back to the fixed exchange rate arrangement. Bordo and Kydland (1995), for example, discuss the gold standard period in terms of such a model of rules with contingencies. As such contingencies they consider wars and financial crises.

This approach has its problems as well (Giovannini 1993a; Hefeker 1996a). The underlying question is to what extent exchange rates can substitute for internal mechanisms to achieve credibility of stable monetary policy. Why should an exchange rate rule be more credible than an internal money-stock growth rule? In other words, why should a policy of pegging the currency to a low-inflation country be more reliable than a policy of maintaining a low growth rate for the domestic money stock under floating rates?

One reason could be that an exchange rate rule is more easy to observe and more transparent. An exchange rate can fluctuate within a band around its peg, but a change in the peg itself is easily detected while it might be much harder to detect a change in the commitment to price stability. Moreover, it is much easier to fix responsibility for a change in the exchange rate because the choice of the regime is policy determined. However, all these observations bear on accountability rather than credibility. A commitment to an exchange peg is not more credible unless its abandonment is more costly than to abandon a promise not to inflate (Kenen 1994). Moreover, if a country is willing to join a fixed exchange rate regime to import credibility, why does it not have the political will to appoint its own "conservative" central banker (Begg and Wyplosz 1987)?[10]

For exchange rates to be a more credible rule than internal rules, two conditions have to be fulfilled. First, the exchange rate rule must be really more credible. But a unilateral commitment of one country to an exchange rate peg is nothing more than just a promise or a declaration of good intentions. Unless there are larger costs in an international breach of a promise than in a national constext there is no difference. As such costs, usually some "political" costs are cited (Melitz 1988) but it is not at all clear what those should be and why they should be higher than, for example, in the case of a breach of an internal money-stock growth rule. Still, it is often argued that especially the EMS is such an arrangement whose abandonment is extremely costly in political terms.

The second condition for the superiority of an exchange rate rule is that the international monetary system has a built-in stabilizer which excludes international and coordinated inflation. The potential danger with central bank cooperation, however, is that it can make the credibility problem of the central bank *vis-à-vis* the private sector even worse. International monetary cooperation may raise the public's expectation of inflation because wage setters realize that a non-cooperative central bank behavior contains a check on each central bank. Hence cooperation may remove this disincentive to inflate. Policymakers could very well be tempted to abuse the exchange rate peg to inflate in a coordinated action (Rogoff 1985a). If countries would inflate jointly, no exchange rate effect could be seen.

Thus, it is not obvious that the exchange rate peg is a better solution to the trade-off between credibility and flexibility as the literature on monetary policy design claims. The monetary policy discussion for the closed economy, instead, has produced much better theoretical solutions than such a simple rule. The exchange rate rule is inferior to a number of alternative solutions, such as monetary targets or contingent contracts for central bankers that punish central bankers directly for deviations from announced money supply targets (Grüner and Hefeker 1995). Additionally, Flood and Mussa (1994), among others, have compared a variety of simulation models and conclude that direct income targeting is much more successful in terms of output stabilization than the exchange rate target. Also, an internal rule excludes the danger of destabilizing speculation that arises under fixed rates and divergent monetary policies.

The credibility based argumentation, finally, never asked what other criteria might help a country to assess whether to peg to another currency or not. Neither was it discussed what would be the optimal currency to peg to. If countries were to peg for importing credibility and stability, the question is why they do not choose the Japanese yen or Swiss franc to peg to, because these currencies are more successful in terms of stability than the widely chosen deutsche mark or the dollar. Thus, this approach is one-dimensional and neglects real factors which help determine the choice of the anchor currency.

The common problem of the Keynesian and the rational expectations literature discussed so far is the basic assumption of a welfare-maximizing government choosing an exchange rate regime which benefits all citizens. Distributional conflicts arising from exchange rate regime choice are neglected since the discussion is often framed in terms of a one-good economy. Relaxing this assumption and adopting a view of policy making where politicians are not welfare-maximizing but self-interested, the distributional effects of fixed and flexible exchange rate regimes become important: who is to benefit from either regime, and how do these interests gain influence on economic policy?

2.2. The Political Economy Approach

Until very recently, the main stream of the theory of economic policy dealt with the economic consequences of given rules. Knowing these consequences and the policy objectives, one could easily derive the optimal policy rule. Implicit to this policy design, however, is a certain view of the policymaker. He is a passive agent which is programmed like a machine (Persson and Tabellini 1990). Once the optimal rule is identified, the policymaker implements it and the private sector adapts to it. This approach to the analysis of economic policy contrasts sharply with the way policy is carried out in practice. The policymaker in reality is an as rational and maximizing agent as any other agent. He responds to incentives and constraints just like the rest of the economy.

This does not automatically mean that the outcome is suboptimal for voters. In a democracy, where all voters are perfectly informed, that is they know the platforms of all the parties and how those platforms, if implemented, would affect their own well-being, and where all parties, in turn, know the preferences of the voters, and where both sides are rational and utility-maximizing, one would arrive at the conclusion that the median-voter's preferences determine the policy-outcome (see Ursprung 1991). If voters' preferences are single-peaked in an uni-dimensional framework, this gives one unique Nash-equilibrium, which is, furthermore convergent. All candidates will converge one the platform which maximizes the median-voter's utility.

It is obvious that those requirements are hardly fulfilled in reality. Information costs and multi-dimensional policy platforms, like party-programs, make the conditions of the median-voter model likely not to be fulfilled. In fact, it seems more appropriate to look for alternative models to explain the political process where politicians have more leeway and where policy platforms of political parties do diverge.

How discretion in the setting of policy is exercised depends upon the motives of policymakers. Acknowledging the political self-interest motives of politicians, discretion in economic policy is predicted to be exercised in a way which maximizes a political objective, such as the probability of reelection. Political support motives then underlie economic policy decisions (Hillman 1989). At an abstract level, this approach can be described as the analysis of a principal-agent problem, with many principals and possibly more than one agent. The individual citizens are the principals. They act politically as well as economically. In their political role, they delegate the formulation of economic policy to an agent (or to several agents), the policymaker(s). The agent in turn selects a policy that maximizes his objectives, subject to the relevant constraints. These constraints include the private economic responses to the policy that the principals choose in their role as economic actors.

Problems arise whenever there is a conflict of interests between the citizens and the policymaker because of disagreement over the final goals of policy. Ultimately, the sources of this disagreement derive from heterogeneity among the citizens that leads them to evaluate differently the effects of particular policies. The role of political institutions is to aggregate somehow these conflicting interests into actual policy decisions. Typically, different political institutions are not neutral in that they induce different equilibrium policy choices. That is, different institutions impose different political constraints on policymakers.

One example of political institutions that influence the policymaker's incentives is the appointment of government through democratic elections. In what follows, voting on candidates or on policies is assumed to be the only form of political participation. Although other forms of political involvement, such as lobbying or protesting, are important, they are perhaps less important for macroeconomic policy than for, say, trade policy or regulatory policy. Almost by definition, macroeconomic policy concerns society at large (see Persson and Tabelllini 1990). Therefore, this approach should be able to explain to a large degree actual exchange rate choices made by policymakers.

Political support motives can be formalized by portraying policymakers as pursuing their self-interest by choosing an economic policy to maximize probabilities of reelection subject to the political weights placed on the support of the gainers and losers from a specific policy. The traditional interest group model of endogenous policy determination focuses on the interaction between interest groups and the elected politician or the government. The political-support version, which originated in the theory of regulation (Stigler 1971; Peltzman 1976), describes an elected politician who pursues a policy which maximizes his political support in order to stay in office. Political support is maximized subject to the gains and losses of those directly affected by the policy. The policymaker balances the marginal gain of political support from industry interests who gain from a particular policy against the marginal loss of political support from interests who lose from that policy. The approach is hence one of constrained optimization, in which the economic agents do not interact strategically with the policymaker in the sense of game theory.

It should be noticed that this model has some cooperative features. The cooperative element shows up in that government policy is in accordance with the maximization of a weighted representation of the utilities of different (interest) groups. There are several groups in the society with each having a utility function which enters the government's function with a certain "power weight". The government's objective function is thus the maximization of a composite utility function. As Potters and van Winden (1994) point out, these models are thus formally equivalent to models that hypothesize a benevolent government.

The Political Business Cycle

The most prominent and well established attempt to bring the influence of voters and the ideology of parties into relation with the choice of exchange rate policy is the political business cycle literature.[11] While the main body of this research dates back to the mid-seventies, there has recently been a revival of this topic, triggered by the rational expectations critique to traditional political business and partisan cycles. Since it has been extended to an open-economy setting recently, it is briefly discussed here.

The traditional political business cycle literature, as originated by Nordhaus (1975) and Mac Rae (1977), presumed high information costs on the side of the voters which were henceforth rationally uninformed and judged the incumbent party only by certain representative economic indicators of *past* economic performance. Reelection motivated politicians maximize their reelection probability, dependent on the voters' decreasing memory of past government performance as measured by a few macroeconomic key variables such as the rate of inflation and the rate of unemployment, by manipulating these indicators in preelection periods.[12] Given a Phillips curve trade-off, time paths are generated that lead to maximum electoral support before election day.[13]

This first generation of political business cycle approaches has caused criticisms in two regards. First, voters are seen as being backward looking only, an assumption which is of course not compatible with the rational expectations assumption.[14] A second criticism is that incumbents have no ideological preferences in those models. The so-called partisan cycle literature, pioneered by Hibbs (1977), in contrast argues that economic policies will consistently differ according to whether they are made by a left or a right wing government. Hibbs argues that left wing governments put more priority on the achievement of full employment whereas right wing government are more concerned with monetary stability. Consequently, left wing governments will pursue a more expansive monetary policy, whereas right wing government pursue a more contractionary monetary policy. Cycles in monetary policy follow as governments with different ideologies alternate in office.

This approach has also been extended to incorporate rational expectations. Alesina (1987) has argued that rational voters will expect a shift in the economic policy after elections if the incumbent changes. If election outcomes are subject to some degree of uncertainty and if parties differ in their preferred policy-platforms, the policies chosen by the winning party will have some real effect for some time because policy variations are not perfectly predicted. This supposes short-run after election blips in employment until economic agents have adjusted their expectations. If the right wing party wins, unemployment will temporarily rise and if the left wing wins it will briefly fall. In the rational expectations setting, a change in the government should then of course also produce an exchange rate effect because of a change in monetary policy. Clearly, the more certain the election outcome is, the smaller the jump of the exchange rate after election day should be (Stephan 1994).

The focus of the traditional political business cycle literature has usually been on the closed economy. Those incentives can however also be detected in the manipulation of exchange rates for electoral purposes. Gärtner and Ursprung (1989) have shown how governments can use monetary policy to generate real depreciations before elections to boost output. In non-election periods monetary policy is tightened to account for the public's inflation aversion and to bring back the economy to its original starting point.[15]

Lohmann (1993a) has extended the analysis of partisan cycle interaction to the national and international level. The partisan cycle is absent when left and right cooperate at the national level whereas cooperation at the international level reduces the cycle because the incentive for beggar-my-neighbor policy (aiming at devaluation) is eliminated. There is however an important difference. The conservative government has a higher incentive to cooperate internationally because it dislikes the inflationary bias from beggar-my-neighbor policy more. The opposite is true for the left government. The model also implies that the parties may be worse off under international cooperation. The left wing government loses from international cooperation because the right wing government's deflationary policy is reinforced.

Finally, Milesi-Ferretti (1995b) has introduced the choice of exchange rate regime in a strategic partisan setting. In this approach two parties, left and right, compete for office and are, at the same time though with possibly varying degrees, interested in maximizing aggregate welfare. Voters have an interest in output maximization and are inflation averse. As governments suffer from the time-inconsistency problem, they have an incentive to bind themselves credibly. One way to achieve this is by pegging the exchange rate.[16] The larger the time-inconsistency problem is for a given government, the higher its incentive to peg since this will reduce the inflation bias and increase welfare. Under the assumption that the left wing government is perceived as being more inflation prone, its trade-off for choosing between exchange rate flexibility (for output purposes) and rigidity (to solve the time-inconsistency problem) is a different one than that which the right wing government faces. Moreover, the right wing government, when in office, might be tempted not to peg the exchange rate when uncertain whether it will be reappointed. Although this could ensure that the left wing government cannot inflate after taking office, this might change the election probabilities. If voters expect the left to be more inflationary and do not like this, they will reappoint the right. But if the hands of the left are credibly tied by entering a fixed exchange rate regime, this problem is solved. Thus, by preserving this problem the right might increase its reelection chance. If the incentive to be reelected is high for the right wing government it will not choose to peg the currency although this would be welfare increasing *ex-post* when the left wins the election nonetheless.

In the next part, however, I will disregard partisan objectives and focus on interest groups and their influence on the choice of exchange rate regimes.

2.3. The Interest Group Approach to Monetary Integration

So far the most developed interest group approach to monetary integration is the analysis of bureaucratic self-interests in monetary integration which, however, takes the aim of integration as given (Fratianni and von Hagen 1992; Vaubel 1990). These papers analyze on the one hand the interests of central bankers and derive a collusive interest. In this view monetary union is sought by the central bankers to reduce competition among them in terms of providing the most stable money. Collusion reduces thus the quality of the money as competition declines. On the other hand, some authors interpret the outcome of the design of the common central bank as reflecting the bureaucracies' interests. Central bankers, when drafting their own statute, were successful in maximizing their comfort and reducing their accountability (see Vaubel 1991, on the Delors Report).

Other than bureaucratic interests in monetary integration and especially monetary union are less well developed. The scarce literature on industrial interests is usually based on class conflicts between labor and capital (see Epstein 1991). It is argued that capitalists use fixed exchange rates to discipline workers' wage demands. This is, however, not consistent with reality where most policy positions are taken along industry lines rather than factor lines because adjustment costs induce factor owners to prefer staying in their sector even if long-term income in other sectors might be higher. While Ruland and Viaene (1993) explicitly address the preferred choice of sectors, stakes in their model depend on current account positions and should thus result in frequent changes of the preferred regime for a certain group. This is also true for attempts to derive exchange rate regime choice from traditional Mundell-Fleming models as in Giovannini (1993c). None of these approaches can explain the rather lengthy periods of regimes.

One should not disregard the fact that interest groups are likely to have preferred *levels* of exchange rates as well (see Frieden 1994, and Stephan 1994) and that governments may use exchange rates as a protectionist instrument (Corden 1982). I will almost exclusively focus on the choice of *regimes* nevertheless. This for several reasons. First, risk-averse traders will favor stability more than possible higher gains from higher exchange rate levels. Second, the rather lengthy periods of existence of a given regime suggest that it is regimes that really matter. Thirdly, one can seriously doubt that governments are able to manipulate exchange rates to a preferred level. Not only will other governments retaliate, but capital flows may drive exchange rates to unexpected and unwanted levels.[17] Finally, since this question has been disregarded so far, its analysis is particularly important.

A Basic Model

The assumptions and argumentation will now be made explicit in a model which will be appropriately altered in the chapters that follow. While its general structure will be preserved, it is adjusted to the main focus of the different chapters. Production is assumed to take place in a two-sector economy, where the difference will be made between tradables and non-tradables in what follows or between a sector dominated by state-owned enterprises and a reforming sector (Chapter 7). Obviously distributional conflicts require a basis for this distributional struggle to be about. It will be generally output and profits. A second influence is the public's aversion to inflation. Policy conflicts arise because the government has more aims than instruments at its disposal. Had it more instruments, the problem would merely be one of assignment. Here, it is assumed that the government wants to increase output and to minimize inflation. For most of this book, its only instrument to reach both aims is monetary policy. In Chapter 6 the government loses monetary policy to an independent central bank but can use fiscal policy instead. The model is hence based on the standard reduced form macroeconomic model developed for monetary and exchange rate policy analysis (see e.g. Canzoneri 1985; Cooper 1985; Rogoff 1985a,b).

Output in the tradables sector

$$(2.1) \qquad y_\tau = \gamma \left[m + e \left(1 - \sigma_e^2 \right) \right]$$

is a positive function of a home component and of net-exports. In this short-run model, an increase in money supply m raises the domestic output whenever $0 < \gamma \leq 1$. When γ approaches zero, of course, the output effect of money supply increases approaches zero as well. There is a variety of reasons why money could have short-run output effects though. When prices are sticky, monetary expansion would increase the demand and thus output of the economy when resources are not fully employed. With flexible prices, nominal wage contracts and adjustment costs imply that monetary policy can influence output as well (Blanchard 1990). If wages are sticky, and monetary expansion increases prices, unexpected inflation has a positive supply effect.[18] One might also assume that governments increase output by fiscal expansion and cover those expenditures by money creation, as in De Kock and Grilli (1993).[19]

The second term, a change in the exchange rate e, defined as the domestic currency price of a unit of foreign currency, captures the change in net-exports. A devaluation makes home-produced goods internationally more competitive and increases exports and output. As explained in detail in Chapter 4, profits from and production of exports goods, however, are negatively affected by the costs of hedging and by exchange rate variability; σ_ε^2 ($0 \le \sigma_\varepsilon^2 < 1$) captures their adverse influences.

The exchange rate is given as

$$(2.2) \qquad \frac{e}{\kappa} = \chi(m - m^*).$$

This is an approximation to model the influence of monetary policy on capital movements. An open market purchase of securities (a monetary expansion) would lead to a decline in interest rates. In an open economy, where foreign and home securities are substitutes, holders would shift out of domestic papers into foreign ones. The exchange rate will adjust to lowering the price of home currency, i.e., the home currency devalues when the domestic money supply increases more than in the foreign country. The elasticity of capital flows is measured by χ.

There is, moreover, a policy instrument to influence the responsiveness of capital flows. The parameter κ measures restrictions on capital mobility, where $1 \le \kappa < \infty$. If κ approaches infinity, capital controls ensure that deviations in money supply of the two countries do not affect the exchange rate. $\kappa = 1$ portrays complete capital mobility and the exchange rate reflects instantaneously deviations in money supplies. Its influence will be discussed in detail in Chapter 4.

The change in output in the non-tradables sector

$$(2.3) \qquad y_N = \gamma m$$

is also positively dependent on money supply increases. For simplification, I exclude any substitutional relation between both goods. This excludes many of the distributional conflicts about the level of exchange rates between the two sectors and allows hence to focus on the exchange rate regime choice.

Inflation is determined by

(2.4) $\pi = \phi m$.

where $0 < \phi \leq 1$. Inflation therefore is a function of monetary expansion. Depending on the size of ϕ, money creation translates into prices. There is a variety of reasons why prices might not adjust fully or with a time-lag to monetary expansion (see e.g. Blanchard 1990; Romer 1993).[20]
Finally, the governments objective function is given as

$$(2.5) \qquad V = -\left\{(1-\alpha)\left(y_T - \overline{y}_T\right) + \alpha\left(y_N - \overline{y}_N\right)\right\}^2 - \omega\left(\pi - \overline{\pi}\right)^2 + \lambda B.$$

The government aims to maximize its political support (for details see Chapter 4) and to minimize deviations from target output levels in the two sectors. It also wants to minimize inflation deviation from the target inflation level, which need not necessarily be zero. B stands for any other additional aim than the two economic variables reflecting full employment and inflation. This reflects politicians' self-interests beyond political support from the electorate. They will balance the influences from industrial interest groups and voters with their own aims which might also be partisan objectives or hegemonic interests. For most of the analysis B will be set equal to zero, but it will reappear in Chapters 3, 6 and 7 as an important influential factor in governments' objectives. Political competition between parties is disregarded.

In contrast to many other works in the field of public choice, where the common assumption is that voters are rationally ignorant, voters' interests are important. Especially the movement from "only" fixed exchange rates to a common currency seems to raise widespread public interest for its symbolic importance. This is in striking contrast to, for example, trade policy where no such public interest is discernible. The question is, nevertheless, how much influence these interests can gain or are even manipulated. Throughout this study voters are modeled as being concerned with monetary stability.

In the next section, two influences on this political support function are discussed which have significantly changed during the time-span this study covers. These are the organization of the political process and the influence of different groups in it, and the degree of capital controls.

2.4. Changes over Time

Two important changes over time must be taken into account when comparing nineteenth century developments and current events. First, there were important political changes. The late nineteenth-century gold standard operated smoothly because of the flexibility of markets, which allowed rapid adjustment to shocks, and because of the credibility of governments' commitment to the maintenance of the prevailing gold parities and the fixed exchange rates they implied. The kind of pressure twentieth-century governments experienced to subordinate currency stability to other objectives was not a feature of the nineteenth-century world, because there was not yet a theory of the relationship between central bank policy and economic fluctuations. In addition, those who suffered from unemployment were not in a position to make their objections felt. For these reasons, the priority that central banks attached to the maintenance of gold convertibility was rarely challenged. Governments only suspended gold convertibility for restricted time periods when large external financial needs arose.

Come the twentieth century, these circumstances were transformed. It was no longer certain that, when the goals of currency stability and full employment clashed, the authorities would opt for the former. Long-term contracts, internal labor markets and bureaucratized industrial relations reduced the flexibility of wages and prices, intensifying the pressures on monetary authorities to respond to employment fluctuations. Universal male suffrage, trade unionism and parliamentary labor parties politicized policy making and diminished the credibility of exchange rate commitments (Eichengreen 1995). Thus, the politization of monetary policy shifted the focus from the revenue raising motive of money creation, which was important in the nineteenth century, to the output stabilizing role of money. Stable exchange rates became more difficult and less desirable to maintain.[21]

This relates directly to the second factor which changed over time and ultimately explains the desire for monetary union, in addition to just fixed exchange rates. While in the traditional optimum currency area literature fixed exchange rates and monetary union were basically synonymous, with the shift to financial markets determined exchange rates, the focus has come on the credibility of regimes and the effects of speculation.

The Role of Speculation

The destabilizing role of speculation on exchange rates has been formalized by the literature on balance of payments crises. The first generation of these models dates back to the late seventies. Krugman's (1979) seminal article assumed that an exogenous government budget deficit lay at the root of the crisis. Excessively expansionary fiscal policy is financed by creating domestic credit. The authorities announce that they are prepared to peg the exchange rate until reserves reach a specified lower bound (usually set to zero), at which they switch to floating. Thus in Krugman's model, a peg must be abandoned once the pegging nation's foreign reserves run out. The finding was that investors inevitably attack the currency *before* reserves are fully depleted and purchase all remaining reserves at that moment. This literature shifted the focus to the potential role of capital flows as becoming destabilizing rather than stabilizing as they had been under the gold standard, but it did not explicitly consider the role of policymakers. Their role is analyzed in another approach.

The second generation of speculative attack models formalized possibilities of self-fulfilling attacks (Flood and Garber 1984; Obstfeld 1986). In these models, multiple equilibria exist in the foreign exchange market because of the contingent nature of the authorities' policy rule. In the absence of an attack, monetary and fiscal policies are in balance and nothing prevents the maintenance of the peg. If and only if attacked, however, the authorities switch to more accommodating policies consistent with a lower level for the exchange rate. Hence, speculative attacks can be self-fulfilling.

This second generation hence brings in the behavior of the government because this makes the speculation self-fulfilling. As Obstfeld and Rogoff (1995) argue, it is a common misperception that capital markets have grown too large for any country to contemplate fixing its exchange rate. Although the volume of daily financial transactions exceeds 1 trillion US-dollars, a number far greater than the reserves of any central bank, there is no insurmountable *technical* obstacle to fixing exchange rates. In contrast, most central banks have access to enough foreign exchange resources to beat down a speculative attack of *any* magnitude, provided they are willing to subordinate all other goals of monetary policy.

Thus, a government is able to fend off a major speculative attack if the monetary authority is prepared to allow a sharp rise in domestic interest rate, especially short-term rates. In general, governments have several options that can be exercised in defense of a currency peg, including borrowing foreign reserves, raising interest rates, reducing government's borrowing requirements and raising or tightening exchange controls. These strategies, if followed to the limit, have some chance of success. But they are painful, especially when unemployment is high and the public and the private sector are vulnerable to high *ex-post* real rates of interest. Governments will therefore balance the costs of such defenses against the benefit of resisting realignment pressures. Often they will conclude that the pain is not worth the gain.

If the ratio of public debt to the national income is high, high interest rates may so raise the costs of debt service that currency traders have reason to anticipate that the authorities will ultimately abandon their policies of monetary stringency once the debt burden raises beyond sustainable heights. If the banking system is fragile, traders may anticipate that interest rates will so weaken the banks that the government will be forced to shift to an expansionary monetary policy to avoid a banking collapse. If high interest rates have an adverse effect on the housing market, one might expect that the government may be forced to a policy shift as well. Finally, economic activity in general may suffer from high interest rates.[22]

When governments determine their resistance on a cost-benefit analysis, self-fulfilling crises become more likely in situations where economic distress already places them under pressure. The reason is that the cost of resisting an attack depends in part on endogenous variables. If markets expect devaluations, interest rates will rise, thus creating an incentive to devalue. Likewise, expectations of devaluation might be incorporated in wage demands, raising authorities' incentives to accommodate. These processes are circular, their timing is basically arbitrary and they can be brought into play by seemingly minor events (Obstfeld 1994). Any economic event that raises the market's estimation of the government's susceptibility to pain, or that lowers the perceived gains from a successful parity defense, can trigger a speculative attack. A recent proposal to avoid such speculative attacks is the reintroduction of capital controls.

The Role of Capital Controls

There has recently began a debate about the effectiveness of capital controls in the operation of pegged exchange rate systems. Wyplosz (1986) and Giovannini (1989), for instance, have argued that controls played an important role in virtually all systems of pegged rates after the second World War. In this view, controls reconciled a modicum of policy autonomy with the commitment to pegged rates, provided breathing space for the authorities to organize an orderly realignment, and made it easier to rebuff speculative attacks not justified by the fundamentals. Gros (1992) and Gros and Thygesen (1992) in contrast have argued that capital controls were always easy to evade and never played a major role in limiting exchange rate flexibility.

In the European context this idea has been revived after the collapse of the EMS, that has been attributed to the markets, referring to "destabilizing speculation". It is thought that speculation on short-term capital movements has brought down the EMS which could have survived in its old form, absent these "hot money" flows (Eichengreen and Wyplosz 1993). Thus a tax for short-term capital inflows in form of interest free deposits with the central bank, additional prudential bank capital requirements against foreign exchange positions, or a tax on gross foreign exchange transactions have been proposed to ensure an orderly movement from the EMS to EMU.[23]

Capital flow liberalization thus makes pegged exchange rates no longer sufficient for stable currency relations. Democratization has brought the politicization of monetary policy and hence uncertainty about the authorities' determination to maintain a currency peg. With technical progress comes greater difficulty of insulating financial markets from capital flows. Thus changes in the political and technical environment lead inevitably to capital flows which are able to topple every currency peg. The choice for policymakers thus becomes starker and eventually one between full monetary union or floating exchange rates. Every arrangement in between these extremes becomes inherently unstable and risks collapse (Corden 1994; Eichengreen 1995).

Notes

1. There is also a large political science literature on this question. For overviews see Eichengreen and Frieden (1993) and Willett (1996), who also criticize that literature for either modeling the state as an unitary actor or for focusing on Marxian conflicts between labor and capital.

2. Although attempts date back more than 30 years, Krugman (1993: 3-4) recognized recently:

We have some suggestive phrases...to describe what we think are the benefits of fixed rates and common currencies...What we do not have, however, is anything we can properly call a model of the benefits of fixed rates and common currencies...I would suggest that the issue of optimum currency areas, or, more broadly, that of choosing an exchange regime, should be regarded as the central intellectual question of international monetary economics.

3. This evidence is summarized in De Grauwe (1994).

4. There has recently been a revival of this literature, based on the discussion about EMU. Recent contributions include Bayoumi (1994), Bofinger (1994), Melitz (1993), Wihlborg and Willett (1991). The classic surveys are Ishiyama (1975) and Tower and Willett (1976). Recent surveys are Corden (1993), De Grauwe (1994) and Masson and Taylor (1993).

5. These are the network externalities referred to above.

6. Horn and Persson (1988), however, have shown theoretically that fixed exchange rates can discipline workers' wage setting behavior, thus leading to more wage flexibility.

7. For empirical surveys on this problem, see Bini-Smaghi and Vori (1992), De Grauwe (1994) and Eichengreen (1993a).

8. The "new macroeconomics revolution" and the introduction of rational expectations have theoretically dismissed money and exchange rate illusion.

9. Collins and Giavazzi (1993) report more inflation aversion for Italy and France developing during the 1980s and *less* inflation aversion in Germany. Growing rates of unemployment may be one reason for this unexpected shift in preferences in Germany.

10. This term has be coined by Rogoff (1985b). He suggested to appoint a central banker who is more inflation averse (conservative) than society to solve the time-inconsistency problem in monetary policy.

11. For a comprehensive overview, see the papers collected in Willett (1988).

12. Frey and Schneider (1981) have qualified this idea by stating that governments only pursue this policy if their popularity is below a threshold level where they risk their reelection if no action is taken.

13. This assumes of course that the government has perfect control over monetary policy outcomes.

14. The evidence is, nevertheless, as Persson and Tabellini (1990, 79) put it "mildly consistent with the predictions" of this naive view. Theoretically, the political business cycle theory can be saved even with rational expectations when voters are imperfectly informed about the competence of candidates (Rogoff 1990, and Rogoff and Sibert 1988).

15. If a J-Curve effect is present, the behavior of monetary policy might be changed (Stephan 1994; van der Ploeg 1989). The inflation rate may even show a trough before elections as appreciations are targeted by the government. A decrease in the inflation rate is generated before elections which, given the short-run demand elasticities, leads to an output boost.

16. Note that this theory is subject to the criticism to this approach put forward above.

17. This point will be taken up at the end of this chapter. Negative effects of speculation on exchange rate stability have already been reason for concern in the last century. The universal gold standard was seen as one way to avoid those speculations (Gallarotti 1993). The problem returned in the interwar years (Nurkse 1944) and was one major concern in the discussions leading to the establishment of the International Monetary Fund (James 1995).

18. Rational expectations do, of course, undermine the efficacy of monetary policy. In that case, monetary expansion might still work as a mechanism to coordinate real wage cuts. This is comparable to Friedman's (1953) "daylight savings time" argument for exchange rate changes.

19. This models does obviously assume that governments or central banks are in total control of the money supply. It also disregards money demand shocks which undermine the controlability of the monetary aggregates.

20. When $\chi > \phi$, one could expect an overshooting effect. Exchange rates would react immediately to monetary expansions while prices would follow later.

21. This was also accompanied by a change in the model with which policymakers operated the economy (Eichengreen 1995; Temin 1989). The Keynesian revolution surely contributed to this change in perceptions of what economic policy is able to provide. The experiences of the 1930s depression and the subsequent recovery through abandoning the gold standard and adopting expansive monetary policy were evidence enough.

22. These crises are modeled, among others, by Bensaid and Jeanne (1994), Ozkan and Sutherland (1994), and Obstfeld (1994) especially in reference to the 1992-93 EMS

crises. Hefeker (1994) focuses on the incentives of a support maximizing government to abandon the peg.

23. The proposal is due to Eichengreen and Wyplosz (1993). See also the critique by Garber and Taylor (1995) and Kenen (1995a).

3

Monetary Integration in the XIXth Century

3.1. Introduction

There is a yet unresolved conflict whether economic interests determine political actions or whether economic behavior adjusts to politically determined situations. In this chapter, it is shown that a combination of both approaches is necessary to understand nineteenth-century national and supranational monetary integration.[1] The national cases of Switzerland, Italy and Germany are presented as examples for successful attempts, and the supranational Austro-German Monetary Union, Latin Monetary Union and Scandinavian Monetary Union as examples for failures.[2] Given that international actions are influenced by national interest groups, the question is what interests are behind early attempts to monetary integration, and what makes them successful or fail?

The historical evidence offers several conclusions. First, the movement towards the introduction of a single currency was determined by an implicit coalition of economic and political interests. In contrast to the EMU case, the nineteenth century was still characterized by power politics of the state and the hegemonic interest of the dominant powers, like Prussia and France. These political interests, seeking hegemonic dominance over other political entities, were supported by economic interests which derive from trade integration. Reduced interests in trade integration, or return to protectionism, then severely undermined the movement towards monetary integration.

Secondly, states and nations will engage in competitive monetary issuing whenever not restricted from doing so.[3] For them to abstain from this requires another source of finance or some compensation. Compensation, however, might sometimes not be sufficient for viable monetary integration. External shocks, as they raise the fiscal needs of governments, may render compensation insufficient and states might resort to monetary financing. It follows, third, that monetary cooperation among states or nations requires an enforceable and credible coordination mechanism to be viable. If this is absent, international cooperation will break down. Thus, one single regulating monetary authority is needed. This basically also explains the difference between successful national integration and failed supranational integration. In the latter cases there were neither sufficient compensation nor the constitutional solution of a common central bank.

These conclusions also suggest that the standard public choice interpretation of integration as collusive behavior among states and monetary authorities to restrict competition is not applicable to the case of nineteenth century monetary integration. Instead, the former independent states and monetary issuing institutions were the ones which most vigorously opposed monetary integration because they feared losing their independent source of profits and finance. In the national cases they thus had to be forced into monetary union. In the supranational cases the cartel interpretation is just as unconvincing since no provisions were made to secure the stability of a possible cartel.[4]

The cases considered in this chapter also clarify that the politically feasible monetary union was in no manner similar to the optimum currency area concept. Instead, a large amount of compensation was involved to make the costs of integration bearable for losers. The politically optimal or feasible currency area was thus more determined by financial power, political will of redistribution and compensation than by efficiency.[5]

Finally, notice that the model underlying the argumentation in this chapter differs in some regards from the one developed in Chapter 2. Conflicts arise between traders who favor stable exchange rates and banks and sovereign heads of state that favor instead monetary autonomy. However, it is not the stabilizing role of money but rather its budgetary role which is contested here. And the political aim of governments (see equation 2.5) is of special importance in this chapter.

The chapter proceeds as follows. I first describe the coalition between political hegemony and free trade interests before turning to monetary integration in Switzerland, Italy and Germany. In Section 3.3, it is shown how monetary integration followed the trade pattern and how another coalition between sovereign states and money issuing institutions opposed common regulation and how this resistance could be overcome. In Section 3.4, I turn to the supranational attempts to monetary integration in the Austro-German Monetary Union, the Latin Monetary Union (France, Italy, Switzerland, Belgium) and the Scandinavian Monetary Union (Norway, Sweden, Denmark). The breakdown in the free trade movement is portrayed, giving rise, in combination with hegemonic decline, to the breakdown of the nationally successful coalition in supranational perspective.

3.2. Political Aims and Economic Integration

This section argues that the economic desire for monetary integration in the nineteenth century was mainly driven by trade integration. The economic interests, however, would probably not have been able to succeed without the support of the political hegemony interest.[6] Economic and monetary integration was seen and used as a vehicle for hegemonic extension, leading to the formation of customs unions and subsequent monetary integration.[7] While monetary integration in ancient history had foremost been a byproduct of hegemonic extension alone, for which the Roman empire might be an example (Trimborn 1931; Veit 1969), in the nineteenth century economic interests in general became increasingly influential in the course of the industrial and *bourgeois* revolution. The restructuring of economies towards manufacturing enlarged the sector of tradable goods considerably (see Pollard 1981). Although this progress had been continuing for nearly three centuries, it accelerated towards the end of the eighteenth and the beginning of the nineteenth century (Bartel 1974). While the political philosophy of the eighteenth century had been mainly mercantilistic, trade being regarded as a zero-sum-game in the static perspective of mercantilism, thriving industries now no longer accepted restrictive trade policy and thrusted towards economic liberalism. The increasing economic concentration and specialization of industries required increased trade, while the large number of internal customs barriers posed significant obstacles to this process by inducing transportation inefficiency and incurring high costs for both producers and consumers.[8] Hence, there was growing pressure from industrial interests for free trade and monetary unification as increased trade raised the costs of monetary confusion.[9] With sovereignty in monetary matters for every city, state, or region, countries were particularly poorly prepared for the industrial *take-off*.

Free trading Britain was conducive to this free trade movement in two regards. First, because of its economic success, it increasingly became a model for European countries to change policies toward free trade; "progress" now meant unification and industrialization. Secondly, already at the end of the eighteenth century it had made attempts to conduct free trade agreements with continental Europe, which were, however, rejected after the agricultural price decline of 1815. In 1846 Britain started a unilateral tariff reduction with the reversal of the Corn Laws (Irwin 1993). In 1860, this desire finally culminated in the Anglo-French Commercial Treaty leading to a wave of bilateral free trade treaties in continental Europe as well.

The Necessity of Fixed Exchange Rates

To understand the drive for a stable international monetary order in this context requires a short look at the chaotic monetary system of that time. At the outset of the nineteenth century, monetary systems were still dominated by metal currency, circulating freely across borders where currencies were accepted according to their metal value. Gold and silver were the traditional currency metals, however generally not minted in pure form but rather in alloys of decreasing purity. Metal currencies consisted of minted coins, whereby the mint par, i.e., the amount of coins of a certain value the mint would give when receiving a certain weight of metal, was the essential instrument of monetary supply control (De Cecco 1992). The other critical value was the free-market price of silver in terms of gold. Generally, a legal rate of exchange between gold and silver was specified by the authorities. In the resulting bimetallic system, where both metals were legal tender, the legal price ratio was determined by the weights assigned to gold and silver coins. Usually, this legal price ratio was held upright even under changing market conditions. This difference between market and nominal price of a currency gave rise to the so-called Gresham's law.[10] Hence the occurrence of two major gold strikes in the 1850s was to have a profound impact on the world monetary system. In 1848 gold was discovered on the Pacific Coast of North America and within the following three years tremendous deposits were also found in Australia, accompanied by an increased supply from Russian deposits. Thus, gold depreciated considerably against silver. Veit (1969), for instance, shows that the share of gold in the world production of gold and silver rose from 7 percent in the 1840s to 18 percent in the 1850s, and fell subsequently back to 8 percent in the 1870s.

Given the situation of changing gold and silver prices and with decentralized minting where the nominal value of coins was unsecured, traders were eager to reduce the transaction and information costs arising from monetary confusion. Money had only reduced unit of account status while the extensive variety of currencies intercirculating implied high costs, especially in cross-border transactions. Stable exchange rates among currencies were seen as a necessary condition for fostering trade and foreign investment. Traders, hence, were not interested in monetary union *per se* but in a stable currency order and convertible currencies. Convertibility at that time was generally understood as the avoidance of fluctuating exchange rates that would result from severing the fixed link between the national currency and the metal standard (Bloomfield 1959). So they rather looked for mutual acceptance between trading partners than for a commonly issued money (Theurl 1992: 253).

Convertibility was also important to have access to the capital market because it had important credibility effects, signaling a government's commitment to sound budgets, balanced external payments and sustainable volumes of foreign borrowing. This desire culminated in a movement away from bimetallism towards a single gold standard. During the World Coinage Conference of 1867, a single gold standard was nearly unanimously voted and when the dominant trading nations finally turned to gold, smaller states dependent upon them changed to gold as well. One reason for the decision to adopt especially gold might have been that gold convertibility had a special meaning. Eichengreen and Flandreau (1994) argue that banks were particularly inclined to lend to governments that had staked their reputations on the maintenance of gold convertibility. A convertible gold based currency thus promised to enhance a country's access to the international capital markets.

Smaller states thus followed Britain, Germany and France which all sooner or later switched to gold. Earlier, however, the countries' choice of the metal standard was determined by the choice of the country or region with which their transactions were linked. The countries of the "British Area" (Britain, Portugal, Canada, Australia, Egypt) were essentially alone on the gold standard. The "French Area" (the LMU countries) was bimetallic and the "German Area" (the German states, the Netherlands, Austria and Scandinavia) was on silver. Smaller countries followed the monetary and trade hegemony of the larger countries (Gallarotti 1993).

The Coalition for Integration

The desire for trade integration was combined with the desire for political integration as well.[11] In Italy, for example, the movement towards national autonomy was combined with the desire of the regional hegemon Sardinia to substitute earlier occupants. Following the Vienna Congress of 1815, Austria had established itself as the dominant political force in Italy, with most of Italy under its influence, while other sections were dominated by Savoyen. From the 1820s onward, however, forces lobbying for political unification gained recognition. With the help of France, Sardinia was eventually able to force Austria out of Italy. Moreover, the Sardinian Prime Minister Cavour, driven also by the free trade interests (Cafagna 1985: 312), already before national unification in 1861 began to unify the tariff system of Sardinia, using economic integration to reach political dominance.[12] Following the parliamentary elections of 1861, the Kingdom of Italy was propagated and the Sardinian constitution, itself modeled after the French example, was adopted.

Most obvious yet is the combination of political and economic interests in the German customs union (Zollverein) example which illustrates how two dominant powers, Prussia and Austria, extended their political rivalry into the economic sphere (Henderson 1968; Holtfrerich 1989). Prussia saw the Zollverein as an excellent opportunity to extend its political power onto smaller states (Fischer 1960; Helfferich 1894, 1895; Trimborn 1931) although it initiated the Zollverein to unite the various parts of its empire. The move towards customs union was caused by Prussia's desire to substitute internal duties for external tariffs as it, following the restoration of 1815, received new territories in the Rhineland. Since there was no connection between these different sections, the Prussian state wished to unite its territories (Henderson

1968). Moreover, the ruling class of landowners, connected with the production of the main export product grain, was interested in free trade. It was supported in this desire by the merchant communities of the port towns. After a failed attempt to counterbalance Prussia's dominance by forming an alliance with Austria, one by one, the Southern states moved over to the dominant (and more efficient) Prussian Zollverein system. As a compensation, Prussia agreed in the Zollverein Treaty to distribute tariff revenues according to population, receiving only 55 percent of the total. It is said that Prussia sacrificed about two million thalers a year (Kindleberger 1975). By sacrificing tariff revenues and distributing it towards smaller states, Prussia could prevent these states from siding with Austria.[13]

This compensation was necessary since at that time tariffs were a main source of income for most states (Fischer 1960: 67). Until well after 1900, the German Reich did have no direct tax revenue and had to rely to a considerable part on customs revenue (Borchardt 1985). Likewise, the first Swiss constitution of 1848 ruled that the federal authority had to compensate the former tariff receiving cantons by distributing most of its external tariff revenues to the cantons as a compensation (Bickel 1964). The cantons themselves increasingly started to tax income and wealth. Only step by step, from 53 percent of total tariff revenue in 1850 to 16 percent in 1874, was the federal state able to restrict redistribution of tariff revenues to the cantons. The second constitution of 1874 did no longer require the federal state to compensate cantons.

These customs unions were by far no single event but part of a general European trade integration.[14] Other custom unions were formed within the Austrian-Hungarian empire and between Moldavia and Walachia. The British desire to use Europe as a supplier of raw materials and as a market for manufactures prompted it to sign a free-trade treaty with France in 1860. France, in turn, moved to free trade as emperor Napoleon saw the needs of imports and duty free raw materials for industrial development (Mc Keown 1983). This treaty inspired other European countries to seek most favored nation status with France as well, which was attained by the German Zollverein in 1863, and by the later Latin Monetary Union members Belgium (1862), Italy (1863), and Switzerland (1864). Sweden, Norway, Spain, and the Netherlands (1865), as well as Austria (1866) and Portugal (1867), resolved similar treaties with France.[15]

3.3. National Monetary Integration

In this section I describe the national monetary integration in Switzerland, Italy and Germany. First the political and economic interests for unification are derived, taking up the arguments developed above. Then the interests of the opposing coalition are shown, and finally I turn to the constitutional solution of this conflict.

Trade Integration in the Zollverein, Switzerland, and Italy

As a result of the Vienna Congress of 1815, the 35 principalities and 4 free cities of Germany were granted full sovereignty in regulating their own coinage system. In the first decades of the nineteenth century, however, Germany was not only flooded with the various coins issued by the sovereign principalities, but in addition coins of French, Russian, British and Danish origin were in circulation. Not only were the coins of different weights and denominations but they were also based upon completely different standards like the thaler in northern Germany and the gulden in southern Germany. Gold was only used for wholesale commercial transactions and as a store of value.[16] Due to the fiscal needs of the states during the Napoleonic Wars, there was also a considerable amount of paper money circulating in Germany.

The same trading oriented industries and commercial interests which pushed for the Zollverein in the North were successful in the South. Driven by these economic interests, the southern gulden states were first to unify their coinage system. The Munich Coinage Treaty of 1837 prescribed the silver content of the gulden and made it a legal tender in all participating states. One year later, cooperation was extended into the North. In the Dresden Coinage Convention, the northern states of the Zollverein and the southern states agreed to mint thaler and gulden according to common metal-content specifications, to withdraw depreciated coins from circulation, and to restrict the circulation of lower value coins. Nevertheless, the states were not obliged to accept coins from other states as legal tender with the exception of a common *vereinsmünze*. This union coin was created to facilitate the exchange between the thaler and the gulden, as 2 thaler and 3.5 gulden constituted one vereinsmünze. But the common coin did not acquire the significant role intended because its value was too high for everyday business (Holtfrerich 1989). Instead, the Prussian thaler extended its circulation throughout entire Germany and was even accepted in the gulden area of southern Germany, becoming the common coin for all practical purposes. Still, however, the diversity of the small change coins remained a problem. Even though over-issuing was ruled out by the treaty and an obligation to redeem any amount of coins beyond a certain level, the diversity of coins minted before the convention remained unchanged. There was no obligation to withdraw coins issued earlier which were still in circulation.

In the 1860s the tradable goods sector in Germany started pushing for the adoption of a single gold standard and for the unification of the coinage system. Germany, when wanting to trade, had to find a common standard with trading partners. The outcome of the French-German war in 1870/71 and French gold reparations made it then possible for Germany upon unification in 1871 to switch the currency standard to gold. Although silver thalers remained legal tender until 1907, Germany was exclusively on an gold standard for all practical purposes from 1873 onward.

Following the southern German states which, in 1837, adopted the gulden as a standard, the eastern cantons of Switzerland adopted it as well and minted it themselves because their trade was oriented towards this region, while the western cantons which mainly traded with France and Piedmont remained on the French franc standard. This adoption of foreign coins as national units of payments resulted in waves of guldens and francs flooding Switzerland, depending on the actual exchange rate between gulden and franc. Putting an end to this chaos, several plans towards coinage unification were developed in the 1830s. But only after 1848, when Switzerland became a federalist state (Bundesstaat), was it possible to centralize, among other rights, the minting rights.[17]

For there was not yet a common "Swiss nationality" feeling, the creation of a Swiss currency was still ruled out. Because of the dominant French position, its political stability and the franc's status as a world currency, Switzerland adopted a coin with the same value and content as the French coins to help Switzerland's participation in international trade. The parliament (Bundesversammlung), nevertheless, retained the exclusive minting rights and only coins from France, Sardinia, Belgium and Parma received legal tender status in Switzerland.

In Italy likewise, the monetary system before unification was organized along trading lines. Northern Italy oriented itself towards France, while the Bourbon South gravitated towards England. Hence, Piedmont and Parma adhered to the French bimetallic standard while the South was on a pure silver standard. Additionally Austrian and Vatican state coins were in circulation so that by 1859 nearly 90 various coins were counted. Most of the circulating means of payments were coins, only one fifth was paper money. Banking laws in all provinces differed in the regulation of coin emission, metal coverage and banking activities, reflecting the particular needs of the state governments to finance their budgets. Banknotes were only accepted in the states which issued them and had no legal tender beyond their borders.

After Italian unification in 1861, due to the political preponderance of Sardinia, the Banca Nazionale di Sardinia (BN) became the leading bank. As a compensation for that, a side-payment had to be made to Tuscany. Florence became capital of Italy in 1865 in exchange for surrendering its coinage privileges (Fratianni and Spinelli 1985).

The choice of the common metal standard was a disputed issue. The BN opted for a single gold standard, but the dominance of silver coins circulating in southern Italy and the trading relations with countries on a silver standard suggested another decision. A compromise was finally reached by instituting a formal bimetallism. Coins from the time prior to unification were exchanged for new coins, full-valued coins could be emitted privately and without restriction while subsidiary coins were restricted to a certain per capita level. The ratio between gold and silver was legally bound to 1:15.5 in the North, while in the South the market rate prevailed, leading to wide-spread arbitrage.

Budgetary Needs and Seigniorage Revenue

Apart from the bimetallic confusion depicted above, a second reason for the widespread working of Gresham's law was the competitive behavior of states (Redish 1993b).[18] States, for reasons of budget financing, had a tendency to issue currency of which the nominal value was higher than its real value, i.e., subsidiary coins or paper money, to reap seigniorage. While new money was generally accepted in the beginning, the public, after having realized its minor value, later turned to the authorities to convert the subsidiary money into full valued money, exploiting the gap between its real and its nominal value. This depleted the metal reserves of the issuing institutions and to avoid further depletion, the new money then usually received forced legal tender status, i.e., lost its convertibility, beginning to drive out the "good" money, like Gresham's law predicts. As to the full valued money's exit from the country, and the on-going creation of subsidiary coin or paper money, fixed exchange rates were forced to finally be given up and the process to be reversed because with full capital mobility speculation against a currency could not be tamed. Bad money now was driven out of circulation.[19]

In the first phase, when new money was readily accepted, governments had an incentive, especially in a monetary union where coins were mutually accepted, to flood not only their own country with new money but other states as well. Fixed exchange rates therefore provided an excellent opportunity for states to enrich themselves on others' costs by exporting part of the domestic inflation. Were instead all states to restrict their money issuance under a regime of fixed exchange rates, all participating in the treaty could profit from low inflation and reduced transaction costs of international trade at the same time. Thus, international monetary stability under fixed exchange rates can be seen as being subject to an inherent free-rider problem (Casella and Feinstein 1989).

Moreover, seigniorage revenue beside tariff revenues and public debt was a source of budgetary finance, as public finance theory predicts (see Grilli 1989). Thus monetary issuing rights, like former tariff revenues, were defended by the sovereigns of the former independent states to be merged in a single political entity. Following the nation-building process these former independent states not only lost their political influence to a considerable degree but also financial resources. As these sovereigns were particularly interested in keeping their revenue sources and in preserving their leeway for independent spending, they resisted monetary centralization as long as possible. Therefore a political central power had to be developed first, being capable to stepwise withdrawing monetary rights. Even more time was required to develop an efficient tax system to substitute for seigniorage revenue. Only then was it possible to nationalize the monetary system.

Also issuing banks were opposed to common regulation and monetary union. State and private banks were those who actually made a profit from monetary confusion, issuing money, taking a margin when changing money and speculating on the changing relation between silver and gold (De Cecco 1992). During times of bimetallism banks maintained the right to choose which metal to issue or redeem. Banks did not have the legal obligation to convert their notes into one specific metal upon request, but were free to choose between gold and silver. Even in the case of full metal-backing they were able to profit from issuing paper money. When they wanted to discourage redemption, they offered to convert notes into silver, which, because of its low intrinsic value, rendered large conversions troublesome. Moreover, they tended to issue only small notes to reduce the likelihood that these would be presented for conversion into full metal coins. Hence, there was also considerable resistance from private or state banks, which took the central powers some time to overcome (Clough 1964: 41).

These groups opposing monetary integration, which I identify as an implicit coalition, thus had to be compensated by the political central power. The larger hegemonic powers therefore had to "buy" the smaller states into accepting integration.[20] For the time being, and as no other sources existed, the former states were compensated with keeping restricted monetary authority, especially for paper money.[21] These preserved rights, not surprisingly, were used by the states to finance their budgets by printing paper money. Because treaties concerning the monetary relations among former independent states, and later among nations in supranational monetary unions, did not initially cover issuance of paper money but only regulated the minting and metal standards of coins, every state had the means to issue paper money beyond the domestic need and to circulate it into other regions as well.

Thus when in Switzerland, upon unification in 1848, the question of paper money was not touched upon and it was left to the cantons to decide upon note-issuing banks, these took advantage of their freedom, continuing the tradition of using cantonal banks as an instrument to finance their budgets.[22] The problem was aggravated when the so-called monetary crisis of 1870, a coin shortage due to the French gold export prohibition during the French-German war, led to the wide-scale acceptance of paper money in Switzerland. Most of the circulating banknotes were issued by the cantonal banks which attempted to extend their own notes' circulation into other cantons as well. Obviously, banks quickly learned to use the possibilities provided by monetary integration to export their currencies (Veit 1969). Private banks, on the other hand, gradually developed a voluntary clearing system with mutual acceptance of paper money.[23]

Also Italy in its coinage reform left paper money unregulated. In 1861, eight banks had the right to issue banknotes, the Banca Nazionale di Sardinia (BN) being by far the most important.[24] Upon political unification in 1861, other banks were merged with the Banca Nazionale so that in 1866 only six remained, making the BN the natural candidate for becoming the Italian central bank.[25] With the banking act of 1874, the privilege of the remaining six banks to issue banknotes was confirmed but also restricted to have legal tender status only in the region of the respective bank. All those not legalized to emit currency had to leave the market, granting the remaining banks therefore a certain market share. However, as in the Swiss case, the regional banks attempted to extend their notes' circulation into others' regions as well (Sanucci 1989: 266). As all notes nevertheless continued to be traded at par, over-issuance by all banks was even encouraged (Fratianni and Spinelli 1985: 487).

In 1866 Italy took part in the German-Austrian war. Financing the war by far exceeded the national income and the government was forced to take a large loan from the Sardinian National bank. Moreover, the convertibility of paper money was suspended and banknotes received *corso forzoso* status throughout Italy. Not only budgetary needs, however, but also pressure groups stood behind the decision to announce paper currency inconvertibility. The manufacturing industry and agricultural sectors pressed towards inconvertibility, hoping for currency depreciation to discourage imports and promote exports. This coalition was also joined by the BN which was convinced that inconvertibility would support its expansionist program by providing the possibility of issuing paper money unrestricted by reserve requirements. The BN's expansion, moreover, was supported by other banks having to keep its notes as a reserve for own issuing.

The stability of the monetary system in Italy was therefore to a large amount dependent upon the budgetary situation of the government. Accordingly, the deterioration of the budget due to involvement in the war was responsible for the inconvertibility decisions of 1866 and the monetary expansion in 1866-67.[26] Although convertibility could be restored in 1883, because of the banks' competitive note issuance due to the rapid economic development in the 1880s, a banking crisis was evoked. The excessive expansion of credit and banknote circulation triggered a speculative crisis, in which course paper convertibility was again suspended. Since it was clear that the crisis was at least partly attributable to the competitive over-issuance of banknotes, the BN was merged with two Tuscanian banks to form the Banca d' Italia in 1893. Nevertheless, the banks of Naples and Sicily could preserve a certain amount of paper issuance for themselves. In 1894 banknotes again received *corso forzoso* status and now the notes of all remaining banks had legal tender character in entire Italy, being redeemable in national paper money or in coin at market rates only.

National Currency Unification

When the commercial-hegemonic coalition between free-traders and political interests was successful in forming a nation, this also implied overcoming the interests of the banks and sovereign states in the fragmentation of monetary rights. Their revenue-defending interest could be overcome by using side-payments first and finally, after having gradually reduced their power and their resistance, by dissolving the states in the former form. The diverging interests of the former independent states were forced into an "union" (Kronman 1985). By political centralization the interests of any former independent state were merged with that of the others. Moreover, the occurrence of several monetary crises due to over-issuance, at times leading to bank breakdowns, finally gave central powers an excuse to merge independent banks into one central bank and to create a two-tier banking system. To support this process, the central powers began privileging one bank. In Italy and Germany, for example, the banks from the hegemon's territory (Sardinia-Piedmont and Prussia) were being privileged by financing the budget of the central power.[27] All convertibility restrictions for their notes were dropped and their notes were made a reserve currency for the other banks.

Therefore, for instance, the beggar-thy-neighbor behavior of small states was actually the reason for the Prussian government to allow the foundation of the Prussian Bank in 1846 after the small neighbor state of Anhalt-Dessau announced its intention to found a banknote-issuing bank, obviously to mainly serve Prussian customers, thereby reaping seigniorage gains (Holtfrerich 1989). The Prussians followed up on Bavaria and Saxony, who in 1834 and 1838 respectively founded note-issuing banks on the basis of private share capital, however with government management and supervision.

The subsequent regulation of issuing rights again also reflects the industries' interests which had expressed their preferences for a unified regulation of the banknote system too for an extended period of time (Holtfrerich 1989). The changing structure of the currency system towards using paper money implied that this had to be regulated to ensure its stability and reliability also. The competitive over-issuing among the German states in the 1850s affected the trading interests adversely, as the larger states (Prussia, Saxony, Bavaria, Baden, and Württemberg) outlawed payment in notes issued in other states in order to hinder their appropriation of overproportional seigniorage gains. In 1867, the commercial interests were finally successful. The German Federation (Deutscher Bund) empowered its legislature to unify not only the coinage system but also the national paper money and banknote system for the entire territory. In 1870 the federation's legislature outlawed the creation of new banknotes, reserving this right for new federal institutions in its Banknotensperrgesetz. This centralization left the Prussian Bank with the exclusive right for unlimited banknote issuance. The Coinage Act of 1873 then also required all paper money not denominated in marks to be withdrawn from circulation by 1876. This, of course, aimed mainly at the private banks in the small states and paved the way for the dominant role assigned to the Reichsbank. Yet again the central power had to compensate the smaller states for the lost revenue. Of the 184 million marks necessary to replace the old coins of the small states, the Reich paid 120 million marks.[28]

With the Banking Act of 1875, monetary unification was completed. It foresaw the establishment of the Reichsbank on January 1, 1876, and gold convertibility for banknotes. Smaller banks were driven out of business through a provision forbidding the issuing of notes under 100 marks. In 1906 only the larger states still had their own bank.

Resistance to the creation of a common central bank originated mainly from traditionally liberal political circles and from the individual states. Accordingly the federal chamber of the parliament (the Bundesrat), resisted the creation of a common bank. Even the Prussian government was reluctant to make its bank a central bank for seigniorage reasons, only agreeing to sell the bank to the Reich at a considerable price in 1875. It was the national chamber, the Reichstag, that insisted on the idea of a central bank.

Switzerland too experienced cantonal resistance in several attempts to unify monetary authority. In 1874 the Swiss federal government made a first attempt to regulate also the emission of banknotes. Because of cantonal resistance this was rejected in a referendum. The law, however, became valid in 1882. It only determined the rules of banknote emission and the mutual acceptance of banknotes, but did not affect the competitive structure of banknote issuing. Not until 1891 were these rights fully transferred to the central authority and in 1907 a central bank could finally be created. This bank had no limit concerning the emission of notes, but was to maintain full convertibility. World War I, however, suspended the convertibility into metal until 1921. To counterbalance the public's hoarding of money, a huge amount of subsidiary coins was issued (breaking the rules of the Latin Monetary Union) along with state paper money. After 1921 Switzerland also moved towards the adoption of a single gold standard, which was actually established in 1925.

3.4. Supranational Monetary Integration

The impetus for supranational monetary integration can be derived from the same interests and motives as national monetary integration. Political expansion and trade integration were also behind supranational monetary integration. It also, however, provided the same possibility to appropriate resources from other members of a union since decisions concerning circulation and issuing of paper money were in any of the three cases left entirely to the domain of the individual nation (Theurl 1992). When nations thus used paper money to finance chronic budget deficits until it far exceeded the amount of specie, redemption in metal was no longer possible at the official rate. To avoid the depletion of currency reserves, paper money received forced legal tender status at which time Gresham's law began operating. The flooding of other countries with subsidiary coins resulted in overabundance there and although subsidiary coins could be presented for redemption by the sending country, the receiving countries at least temporarily granted a credit to the issuing country.

Over-issuance led to a market devaluation of the currency and eventually to the breakdown of the official exchange rate because exchange rates could not be defended under full capital mobility and without support among the involved central banks.[29] Nevertheless, in case of external shocks like wars, countries frequently resorted to printing money.[30] Taxation, as an alternative, was not yet a developed instrument and the costs of taxation thus high. Moreover, it was unattractive because by printing money, the (inflation) tax had a broader basis and through money export other nations bore the tax burden too.

The following sections describe first the formation of supranational currency areas and then their problems and the reasons for their breakdown are addressed.

The Movement to Free Trade in Western Europe

The first attempt for supranational monetary integration was made between Austria and the Zollverein, being caused by struggle for political leadership. Prussia opposed Austria's participation in the Zollverein, but as a compromise a free trade treaty with Austria was concluded in 1854, setting the stage for negotiations about a common coinage convention for the Zollverein and Austria. Still hoping to join the Zollverein, Austria saw monetary integration as a vehicle to reach this goal by instrumentalizing monetary policy. Prussia instead considered the Austro-German Monetary Union (AGMU) as a way to extend its political power into the adversary's domain.

Having a central banknote monopol since 1816 and being on an inconvertible paper standard since 1848, Austria was expected to reestablish convertibility before negotiations in 1854.[31] Austrian efforts to reach convertibility by selling the railroads and taking a loan on the capital market were thwarted by the outbreak of the Crimean War. For Austria's participation in it, inconvertibility had to be extended. Another problem was the changing relationship between the prices of silver and gold. Austria wished to establish a gold standard in the AGMU, for it assumed that it would be easier to resume specie payment in the at that time relatively cheaper gold. Prussia, however, wished to maintain the silver standard and the dominant position of its thaler. Negotiations broke down over this issue and were only resumed in 1856 when Austria dropped its demand for a common gold standard. In 1857, the Vienna Coinage Treaty was signed between the Zollverein and Austria, in which also Liechtenstein took part.

In the AGMU convention three distinct currencies were linked together by a constant rate of conversion and a common unit of account, the silver mark. At that time (before the German Monetary Union) Prussia and the northern states used the thaler which was valued at 14 to one silver mark, while Bavaria and the southern states used the gulden, which had a value of 24.5. Austria used the gulden as well, but its currency unit was valued slightly higher than the Bavarian one. Although no attempt was made with AGMU to introduce a common currency, provision was made for a common *vereinsthaler* to be the only coin in circulation in all participating states of which a minimum number had to be coined each year providing for the necessary unit of payment. The choice of the thaler as common unit clearly reflects Prussia's preponderance as does the decision to maintain the silver standard. But as in the case of the Dresden coinage convention, the common vereinsmünze was rarely used by the public. Instead the Prussian thaler was used in Austria as well. For external payments a gold-based unit, the krone and half-krone, was created. The price ratio between gold and silver was left to be determined by the market, avoiding the confusion of the bimetallic standard. Another important element was the regulation that as of 1859 all paper money had to be redeemable into silver.

The rising influence of economic interests in forming monetary unions, however, was most visible in the case of the Latin Monetary Union (LMU) constituted by France, Italy, Switzerland and Belgium. Another important reason for the formation of a common currency area stemmed from bimetallism and the problems resulting from changing relative prices of gold and silver. When increasingly silver coins left France due to silver scarceness in neighboring states because of the gold flood after 1848, a shortage of full-value silver coins became virulent because there was virtually no small payment medium left. The government attempted to adjust to the situation by reducing the fine content of silver coins.

Governments generally, having acquired the technique for producing standardized token coins (Redish 1993a), resorted to minting subsidiary coins. When Switzerland also began reducing the fine content of subsidiary coins, the result was a difference in fineness among circulating coins, hindering trade, commerce and travel with the neighboring states Belgium, Switzerland, and Italy, since France in turn was reluctant to accept these coins. It became increasingly apparent that only concerted international action could remedy this situation.[32] Moreover, Napoleon III saw monetary integration as a welcome possibility to extend France's political rule and to maintain the status quo of France's superiority in the monetary system.[33]

Once again, monetary integration followed the trade connections and the formation of the LMU reflects foremost a recognition of existing facts. All of the countries which later formed the Latin Monetary Union traded already heavily with France (Cohen 1993; Flandreau 1993b). When therefore Belgium became independent in 1831, it had already adopted the French monetary system. Its coins were of the same fineness, value and name as the French coins. The French money was even made legal tender in Belgium (Bartel 1974). From 1853 onward, Belgium completely stopped its minting of silver coins, as it was easier to buy the coins (against gold) in France and import them for use (Willis 1901) while full-valued coins were exported to the Netherlands and Germany, exhibiting once again the working of Gresham's law.[34] Switzerland and Italy, as described above, were also already on the French standard, with the French franc as legal tender in both countries too. As the franc circulated in these countries, in turn the national coins of Italy, Belgium, and Switzerland intercirculated among each other. Notice in this context that France was also the main creditor to these countries (Flandreau 1993b). Although these capital flows diminished when the Latin Monetary Union was formed, the other countries now had the possibility to coin the currency to repay their debt.

It was Belgium that actually proposed an international monetary conference in 1865 at which the juridical basis for the Latin Monetary Union was set. Together with the Swiss and the Italian delegations, the Belgian delegation made formal demands for the adoption of a single gold standard but the French replies were reluctant. France instead had augmented large silver depots, preferring thus a standard which included silver. Redish (1993a) suggests that Napoleon might have wanted to use bimetallism as a bargain chip for the International Monetary Conference in 1867, in which he wanted to trade it against the common gold standard being based on the French gold coinage. The French *haute finance* was also very much interested in letting the existing system survive, as bimetallism provided an opportunity for very profitable arbitrage operations by exploiting the gap between currencies' real and nominal values (De Cecco 1992; Veit 1969). Willis (1901: 57-60) argues that the French government was very dependent on the Banque de France, which also preferred bimetallism, to finance its budget deficits, giving the latter thus considerable influence. Finally, because the Banque de France was the only central bank with a reserve strong enough to stabilize the entire area's system, the official French view dominated (De Cecco 1992).[35]

The treaty, conducted for 15 years and renewable, was thus essentially a reinforcement of the status quo in which the contracting parties agreed on uniform standards concerning minting and issuing of gold and silver coins.

However, coins only had mutual legal tender status with public bodies; only in Italy and Switzerland did private subjects have to accept foreign coins also.

Greece was nominally admitted to the LMU and joined it in 1868, but subsequently proved to be a negative achievement because of its unsound financial and economic conditions. During the nineteenth century Greece experienced four episodes of suspension of the convertibility of note issues and except for the first they all happened because of budget problems of the government in response to wartime emergencies (Lazaretou 1995). Later, a bilateral treaty between Austria and France welcomed the inclusion of another important member without formal admission. Spain and Romania also took steps to adopt the franc system, so as of 1880 approximately 18 states were using the French monetary system.[36]

The third attempt to form a monetary union, the Scandinavian Monetary Union (SMU), was initially the most successful. Like the LMU, the SMU was the formal integration of the Norwegian, Danish and Swedish monetary systems among which there already existed an informal intercirculation of coinage. This, the similarity of the economies in general and the high degree of trade dependence turned out to make a rather successful attempt. In this regard, the SMU was nearest to an optimum currency area. While Sweden and Denmark already established the SMU in 1873, due to anti-Swedish sentiments and the wish to demonstrate independence, Norway did not join the LMU before 1875.[37]

To a certain extent, the SMU was a copy of the LMU and also inspired by the ideas of the world coin movement (Trimborn 1931). Following the International Monetary Conference in 1867, Sweden undertook a monetary reform to prepare for an eventual participation in an international monetary union and the adoption of the gold standard. Although all Scandinavian countries first considered taking part in the LMU, the reluctance of France to surrender the bimetallic standard finally deterred the Scandinavian countries from joining because they soon expected the devaluation of silver (Janssen 1911). The close Scandinavian trading and commercial ties with northern Germany and the movement of the German empire to the gold standard again were of significant influence. Norway especially advocated the adoption of the German standard during various conferences on the question of bimetallism or gold.[38]

Finally though, the German currency was rejected as a standard because it was unlikely to become a world currency (Janssen 1911). The common unit of account finally chosen was the crown, consisting of 100 öre, and defined in measure, weight, and fineness according to the Swedish riksdaler. Gold and subsidiary coins differed only in their minting stamp and coins minted in one country were legal tender in the others as well. In contrast to the LMU, in the SMU no limit for the coinage of small coins was set. The contracting parties found it inappropriate to fix the amount of coinage needed in circulation in advance. To avoid mutual exploitation, nevertheless, coins only had legal tender status up to a certain amount and redemption was foreseen into full valued coins upon request as well. This of course greatly enhanced the credibility of the union. No preparations were made for the treaty's dissolution, although the treaty term was subject to prolongation in 1884.

The Return to Protectionism

As argued above, monetary integration was economically most influenced by underlying trade integration. This underlying free trade movement, however, took a dramatic change in the 1870s, when American, Indian, and Russian grain imports and America's development towards industrial superiority (in e.g. fertilizers) deteriorated the European trade balance (Gourevitch 1977; Irwin 1993; Mc Keown 1983; Pollard 1981). This industrial advantage, in combination with reduced transportation costs, rendered Central and Western Europe uncompetitive and exerted considerable price pressures. 1873 remarks a break, after which prices continued to drop for the next two decades, while output continuously rose and although new industries like steel and chemicals sprang up, the return on capital declined.

Increased competition from outside Europe caused breakdowns in domestic industries and raised the level of protection in the concerned countries (Gallarotti 1985). The increased competition from outside Europe led to increased protection in Europe as with declining industries more potential partners were to be found in protectionist efforts because of the industrial depression (see Cassing et al. 1985). Thus the influence of protectionist interest groups triggered non-cooperative behavior of the states, as the objectives of political support maximizing governments changed. The internal political equilibrium changed when the implicit coalition between industry and politics, initially successful on the national level, broke down since traders changed their attitude toward supranational monetary unification. Thus an unholy alliance of industrialists and agriculturists (in Germany doted "the marriage of iron and rye" between junkers and heavy industry) pushed the countries of Europe, with the notable exception of Britain and the Netherlands, towards protectionism (Rogowski 1989).[39] States once again regarded trade as a zero-sum-game, reviving mercantilistic behavior (Pollard 1981: 59) as distributional struggles became more intense.

Customs union and national unification moreover caused an industrial reorientation towards the national level. Although most of the former independent states were initially oriented towards different trading partners and thus probably interested in forming currency areas not along the political lines but rather along trade lines, the movement towards customs unions changed this as the now nationally integrated regions became more attractive as trading partners with the reduction of customs borders. Moreover, as stronger nations developed, becoming more efficient in using central power (taxation, manoeuvring armies etc.) and making centralized power the dominant source of power and patronage, the loyalties and expectations of citizens' were directed towards the national center.

The changing economic conditions in the 1870s and the following wave of protectionism finally changed industries' interests toward using money as a protectionist device through the instrument of devaluation. The emission rights granted to former sovereign states and banks as a compensation for national integration rendered supranational agreements even more difficult.[40]

The Collapse of Monetary Integration

In his classic work on collective action, Olson (1965) suggests two ways to overcome the free-rider problem in international cooperation. One solution is a small group of players, making surveillance possible and defection punishable, while the second solution is asymmetric distribution of power among the participating actors. The so-called hegemon can overcome the cooperation problem (Kindleberger 1986) either by bearing the entire costs for the provision of the public good alone or by coercing the smaller states to bear their share of costs.[41] While in early history hegemons attained this by exercising monetary sovereignty over their entire empire, the nineteenth century instead saw the development toward a balance of power, reducing the dominant role of a hegemon. Hegemonic decline made thus another formula necessary and as Keohane (1984) pointed out, hegemony might be helpful in the erection of a system, but is not enough for its survival. His notion "hegemonic cooperation"-- i.e., that cooperation is required for systemic stability even in periods of hegemonic dominance, although the presence of a hegemon may encourage cooperative behavior-- directly applies to international monetary relations as well.

But in the supranational cases there was neither a constitutional solution nor a dominant power to coerce participants to behave cooperatively. Nations instead preferred to retain political and monetary autonomy. Even the threat of "tit-for-tat", which usually solves prisoners' dilemmas in a repeated game (Axelrod 1984), could not convince the national players to fulfill their agreements. As explained, this is attributable to the occurrence of external shocks, mostly wars, which considerably influenced the time-discount rate of the players.[42] When, moreover, the dissolution of monetary unions became visible, as most supranational monetary union treaties foresaw only a restricted term of duration which had to be prolonged, cooperation broke down .

The AGMU as the most shortlived attempt of supranational monetary integration shows this clearly. Although, the Vienna Treaty was the only nineteenth-century monetary agreement that explicitly touched upon the question of paper currencies, it could not avoid non-cooperative behavior. It ruled out legal tender status for paper money and even required Austria to again reach full convertibility by January 1859. Austria exerted great effort, reaching silver convertibility by September 1859. However, its involvement in the Italian war of independence forced it back to the paper standard. While again coming close to convertibility in 1866, the war against Prussia drove Austria out of the AGMU in 1867.

During the whole period of its existence the AGMU was subject to continuous violations of the treaty by Austria, constantly over-issuing paper money to finance its budget deficits. Due to the working of Gresham' s law coins were thus driven out of Austria to flow into Germany while German thalers were traded with an agio (Veit 1969: 464). Nevertheless, the Austrian minted vereinsthaler maintained legal status in Germany even beyond AGMU dissolution. The acceptance of the Austrian coins posed a severe problem for Germany when it switched to the gold standard in 1871 as silver bullion was transported to Austria and reimported into Germany as coins (Veit 1969: 466). When, in 1874, Austrian coins were forbidden in Germany, the coins made their way into Belgium.

The LMU Treaty in contrast not even tried to address the problem of paper money. It even failed to regulate the relationship between gold and silver. Of course, since fineness, weight, and measure of gold and silver coins were defined, a ratio between the metals was factually determined (1:15.5), reflecting the then market values. But as the respective values of gold and silver frequently changed thereafter, the real exchange rate between silver and gold fluctuated. Already shortly after the formation of the LMU, gold and silver changed drastically the relative values again to the benefit of gold. This was due to the adoption of the gold standard by major trading nations, the increasing role of subsidiary coin, the increase of silver production in America, and finally the growing commercial preference for gold even in those nations on a silver standard. The decline in the relative value of silver urged the member states of the LMU after 1872 to suspend free coinage, because of the flood of silver from third countries due to the relative overpricing of silver at LMU mints, to avoid the depletion of currency reserves.

Once again, the free minting and circulation of 5 francs and larger coins foreseen in the LMU Treaty proved the workings of Greshams's law and provided the possibilities to enrich one country on the costs of others. As the market value of silver at a fineness of 0.835 was below its nominal value in coins, countries had an incentive to buy silver and distribute it in minted form later (Veit 1969: 707). The issue was extensively discussed during several conferences in 1874, 1875, 1876, 1878, 1879, 1885, and 1893 and measures were taken, restricting the amount each state was allowed to mint to 6 franc per capita with the aim of containing the massive over-issuance.[43] For seigniorage reasons, particularly voiced by Italy, a total stop of subsidiary coin minting was not enforceable (Flandreau 1993a), although Switzerland and Belgium advocated the total prohibition of silver minting. France again proposed a per capita restriction. This restriction was partly successful and subsequently brought gold coins back into circulation (Willis 1901). France, on the other hand, began redeeming paper money into silver coins to reduce its vast amount of silver reserves.

When Switzerland finally proposed the dissolution of the treaty, this gave rise to an important amendment to the treaty. The minting of silver subsidiary coins was "temporarily" suspended in 1885 and never again taken up, i.e., the LMU moved to a "limping" gold standard. The parties also agreed that 5 franc coins should be reimbursed by the country that had issued them at the expiration of the treaty. This provision turned out to be a determining factor for the prolonged survival of the LMU. As this massive reimbursement would be too costly, most states were hesitant to leave the LMU despite its problems (Redish 1993a; Theurl 1992).[44]

While the over-issuing of coins was to be checked by the provision of redemption, the issuing of paper money was not regulated at all, leading to different growth rates of note issuing. The starting point was the Italian *corso forzoso* of 1866. As a result of the chronic budget deficit, accompanied by a large trade deficit, Italian authorities increased the circulation of paper money. Not surprisingly the circulation soon reached a point at which a redemption in gold was no longer possible. Coins exited Italy, entering into the other member states where they maintained full value, while paper money depreciated. While the other LMU states were flooded with Italian coins, Italy itself experienced a shortage of coins and, to make matters worse, was forced to redeem them in gold when they were presented. Nevertheless, the other countries involuntarily provided Italy with forced credit to the amount of Italian coins circulating in their regions.

Until World War I this process repeated itself several times in Italy and Greece. Then, however, all countries involved in the war resorted to *cours forcé*. All currencies depreciated against the Swiss franc, leading to massive speculation. Halting intercirculation on the other hand would have meant a formal dissolution of the LMU, which, in fact, came about with the renationalization of coins in 1926.[45]

In contrast to the LMU, and like the AGMU, the SMU made the intercirculation of banknotes possible as well. Although it was not stipulated in the treaty, banknotes, which had much more significance in Scandinavia than in the rest of Europe and thus exceeded coins considerably in circulation, were accepted among the states at par (Theurl 1992). Hefeker (1995b) shows the stability of relative shares of banknote issuing among SMU countries.

In 1879, in a first modification of the treaty, an upper limit for the issuing of subsidiary coins was introduced. In 1888, the most particular feature of SMU was introduced, viz. a clearing union with short-term (3 month) credits to balance current accounts was created. Moreover, in 1894 Sweden and Norway agreed on accepting each others' notes at par. In 1901, the same agreement was introduced between Denmark and Norway.

The stability of the respective currencies and their rates of exchange was certainly a key factor for the success of the SMU as the stability of exchange rates made the continuing intercirculation of notes and the efficient clearing mechanism possible. One reason might be that there already partly existed centralized paper money authorities. There was a long tradition of central banks having banknote monopolies in Denmark and Norway, while in Sweden competitive private issuing banks existed. Paper money was legal tender, however without convertibility.

Another reason for the underlying stability is to be found in the similar economic structures of the three Scandinavian countries. Most importantly, however, the Scandinavian countries were not exerted to a wave of external shocks like the Central European countries. They thus were not forced to resort to monetary financing of their budgets. When this occurred with World War I, the SMU also collapsed. Moreover, none of the countries were host to a financial center so that they were somewhat removed from the stresses and destabilizing capital flows that occurred in international finance. Another important feature for the success of the SMU is the fact that it adopted a single gold standard from the beginning and that banknotes and coins could be redeemed without difficulty, as there were neither external shocks nor budget problems, avoiding any necessity of *cours forcé*. In 1905, however, after the dissolution of the political union with Norway, Sweden cancelled the clearing union treaty because it felt the clearing mechanism was biased against itself. A new, more restrictive treaty was signed, foreseeing a reduced amount of credit facilities.

Again, World War I posed an end to the SMU convention. After the suspension of the gold standard in 1914, money growth rates and price movements began differing. Norway and Denmark could considerably expand their exports in orienting towards other trading partners, which also reduced their interest in SMU. The increased money supplies were gradually transferred to Sweden and finally, after maintaining initially their value because of stable expectations, this led to a depreciation of both currencies against the Swedish currency. (In 1920 the Danish currency was valued at 77.05 and the Norwegian at 80.75 against the Swedish currency [Bergman et al. 1992]). Shielding itself against imported inflation, in 1916 Sweden placed an embargo on gold imports which, however, because of the SMU Treaty, could not be extended to the Norwegian and Danish coins as well. Sweden, thus, ultimately required both to also introduce an embargo, and in February 1916 an agreement was reached which prohibited Norwegian and Danish gold export into Sweden. This agreement, however, broke down in autumn 1916 and only because of the Swedish threat to leave the SMU otherwise could be reintroduced in 1917.[46] Subsidiary coins, nevertheless, continued to be smuggled into Sweden and full-valued coins were stored in Norway and Denmark, illustrating once again the working of Gresham's law. Sweden, on the other hand, attempted to reexport these coins. Finally, fixed exchange rates had to be abandoned and with them the legal tender provisions as well.

3.5. Conclusion

The chapter pointed out that cooperation is necessary beyond the existence of a hegemon to make monetary integration possible. But as nations are subjected to asymmetric shocks and thus changing objectives, their willingness to cooperate is clearly affected. Whether any rules could be binding enough in such a situation is doubtful. Hence a constitutional solution, making free-riding and time-inconsistent behavior impossible, must be applied to monetary integration to be successful.

For this reason, the successful attempts of monetary integration in the nineteenth century are characterized by a more or more less rapid centralization of issuing rights. In Germany and Italy monetary sovereignty was immediately transferred to the central state upon unification of the respective nation, while in Switzerland only the minting rights were transferred. In Germany this process was accompanied by a complete currency reform, while in Switzerland and Italy it was restricted to a coinage reform in which the states maintained the rights to emit banknotes. But only with reductions of the monetary sovereignties of private banks was it possible to overcome the diverging interests of former independent states and to finally nationalize the monetary system.

The supranational unions, on the other hand, all followed a similar pattern of creation, adaptation, and dissolution. All treaties have in common that they started with a partial intercirculation already existent in border regions based on trading relations, so that monetary integration was partially already existent before monetary union. However, these unions only encompassed part of the monetary system, leaving space for national economic considerations. The absence of a constitutional regulation proved devastating to the system in case of external shocks. In addition, the change in the monetary structure toward paper money meant a broadening of the operation set for every member, as a larger part of the circulating money became independent of common regulation, allowing mutual exploitation. In each case, fixed exchange rates were agreed upon, but were not subject to later realignments, causing thus the real and the official exchange rate to differ. On the other side, treaties were not flexible enough to manage external shocks and made it thus even more attractive to break the rules, as violations of conventions were in no case subject to penalties. Adaptations made to the treaties were first designed to save the system, later, however, to avoid the unfavorable outcomes of dissolution. The entire process of supranational monetary union hence went from supranationalization of money back to renationalization (Theurl 1992: 241), as the major repercussions of external shocks and the changing commercial interests shaped the behavior of nations. Moreover, national unifications' own problems, privileges, and side-payments were underlying the process of supranational integration. While is was necessary to grant these favors, they endangered the supranational unions.

Notes

1. I use monetary integration in this chapter to describe arrangements with fixed exchange rates between states, where at least part of each others currencies have legal tender status. For alternative definitions, see Chapter 2.

2. Surveys on nineteenth-century monetary integration can be found in Bartel (1974), De Cecco (1992), Janssen (1911), Krämer (1971) and Veit (1969). Theurl (1992) provides the most detailed and comprehensive account.

3. Rolnick, Smith and Weber (1994) in their study of the origin of monetary union in the U.S. describe the same behavior. Exchange rate variability being viewed as costly gave rise to attempts of monetary union. State power to money creation posed the problem of competitive money issuing and only taking away this power from the states solved the problem.

4. While cartels are usually plagued by stability problems, I would argue that it was not even tried to form a cartel in the context considered here.

5. Fiscal integration and compensation is of course also a widely discussed issue in today's attempt to form a European monetary union. See e.g. Kenen (1992), Sala-i-Martin and Sachs (1992).

6. The role of ideology will not be considered as a decisive factor behind politics, although it might have had a certain influence. I regard the cultural and ideological idea of unity to be non-decisive unless supported by other interests. Moreover, I find it appropriate to disregard citizens' interests, as in the nineteenth century democracy was not yet widely established and citizens had only little political influence (see Chapter 2).

7. The Swiss case and the Scandinavian Monetary Union instead are rare examples in which nearly equally powerful states united. This, however, is no surprise as one might also expect small states to form a union among themselves rather than joining larger powers (Bernholz 1985). Moreover, the theory of international relations illustrates that it is possible for a group of

countries to substitute the hegemon and to provide stability themselves (Snidal 1985).

8. In the later united Germany alone, for example, there were 1,800 customs barriers at that time.

9. The desire by industry for free trade was not unambiguous. There were industries which rather preferred some protection and others that opposed liberalization altogether. Different degrees of free trade are not considered here, however. For details, see Henderson (1968) or Irwin (1993).

10. This term is used to describe the situation under fixed exchange rates where the coins with smaller metal value will drive the coins with higher value out of circulation because these are either hoarded, exported and used abroad with an agio, or melted and sold at metal value. When the market price differed substantially from the legal ratio, only the metal that was cheaper at the market price would be brought to the mints (Friedman 1990). See Rolnick and Weber (1986) for a detailed specification of the conditions under which Gresham's law holds. I return to its working below.

11. There is a vivid discussion of what is first, monetary or political union. While the Bundesbank for obvious reasons argues that political union has to come first (see Chapter 6), Holtfrerich (1993) makes a strong case for the opposite based on the German example.

12. After Italian unification the Sardinian tariff system was extended to entire Italy (Clough 1964: 40).

13. However, for fear of foreign retaliation and exporter interests, the level of the external duties was considerably lowered (Pollard 1981: 28). In fact, from 1818 on, Prussia had the lowest level of tariffs in Europe. One more reason to lower tariffs was to keep Austria out of the Zollverein (Mc Keown 1983).

14. See Viner (1950) for a comprehensive overview of customs unions in theoretical and historical perspective.

15. All of these developments toward free trade were particularly supported by an evolving transportation system. Especially the development and rapid growth of railway traffic and the interconnection via rivers lowered considerably the costs of transportation. Later, however, reduced transportation costs would also contribute to the revival of protectionism. Free capital movements were also a determining factor in economic interconnectedness, with London, Paris, Hamburg, Amsterdam, and Basel as European financial centers.

16. Only Bremen, through its oversea connections, operated on a gold standard.

17. Subsequent negotiations among cantons concerning monetary reform were, however, not concerned with paper money since this was deemed to be solely of minor importance. At that time banknote issuing was not profitable as

notes had to be fully convertible and redeemable on a 100 percent metal basis. They had no legal tender status and were solely accepted by the issuing banks themselves.

18. I will use "state" to describe smaller communities to later merge to form a "nation". Thus, the cantons of Switzerland will be called states while the united Switzerland will be called a nation.

19. Bernholz (1989) named this reversal of Gresham's law Thier's law.

20. Casella (1992b) argues that small states generally have to be compensated with a overproportional share of the seigniorage. They have to be "bribed" into the monetary union. In the cases considered here a combination of seigniorage and fiscal redistribution was used. In the Italian case, for instance, the central power also took on the debt of the sovereign states upon unification (Clough 1964: 43).

21. There is, however, no proof that the nonregulation of paper money at the outset of monetary unions encompassed a bargain between the central power and the states and was not simply due to ignorance. The fact, although, that there were already voices demanding the regulation of paper money, recognizing the problem (Trimborn 1931: 69), indicates that it actually did involve a bargain. This bargain was necessary to avoid a recurrent breakdown of the union, having the same side-payment role as tariff revenue redistribution.

22. Moreover, banks were seen as a political instrument, as, for instance, two rivalry banks affiliated with the liberal-radicals and the aristocrats were founded in Geneva in the 1840s (Weber 1988: 473).

23. This, however, can also be viewed as an attempt to avoid a federal regulation (Theurl 1992: 77). In fact, banks broke cooperation whenever deemed necessary.

24. Between 1848 and 1851 and again in 1859 the BN had already emitted money with forced legal tender status (corso forzoso) to finance the fiscal needs of Sardinia.

25. Even before the coinage reform of 1861 an attempt was made to unify the issuing of paper money with the BN. Parliament blocked this initiative for the obvious reason not to lose the monetary sovereignty of states.

26. The second source for government finance was the Parisian capital market. Because of a remarkable price difference for governments bonds in Italy and Paris, however, speculative capital flows destabilized the exchange rates and deemed the intended stability of exchange rates in the Latin Monetary Union obsolete.

27. Goodhart (1988: 19) interprets this as a contract between central bank and nation by exchanging banking monopoly for seigniorage. Since some central banks, however, were state-owned, this is nothing less than an appropriation of rents and their securement in a monopoly position by the

central power. In the case of private central banks, it is an allocation of rents to those private interests.

28. The compensation was actually paid by the Reichsbank.

29. Flandreau (1993b) argues that the Banque de France was unwilling to act as a lender-of-last resort to the Latin Monetary Union. Kindleberger (1986) derives the necessity of a lender-of-last-resort for the stability of the international monetary system.

30. De Kock and Grilli (1993) derive theoretical arguments for exchange rate regime switches and fiscal autonomy for large external shocks. Bordo and Kydland (1995) also derive the benefits of "escape clauses" for large shocks. Thus for them the collapse of exchange rate regimes is due to welfare considerations of a government. For a critique of this approach, see Chapter 2.

31. Hefeker (1995b) and Theurl (1992) show how differently structured the monetary systems in Austria and Germany were, already indicating the problems which were to follow.

32. According to Veit (1969: 701) the true reason behind the LMU was less the healing of the fragmentation of coinage, but rather the avoidance of its ongoing deterioration.

33. De Cecco (1992) views the LMU as an indirect outcome of the Napoleonic empire as Napoleon was successful in preserving French economic and financial hegemony.

34. In 1860 the coin circulation in Belgium was 87 percent of French origin. Gold was widely used too, but its non-legal tender character and the overly large denominations created difficulties for daily transactions.

35. The smaller states were also interested in convincing other nations to join the LMU (particularly Britain) which had required a gold standard, but feared the costs which would be prompted by a substitution of silver coins for gold (Willis 1901). This might be another reason why they finally accepted the French position.

36. Dubois (1950: 11) names Bulgaria, Serbia, Finland, Crete and a majority of South and Central American republics.

37. This is somewhat surprising since Norway and Sweden also formed a political union from 1814 to 1905. Nationalism might on the other hand be the explanation for this reluctance. The influence of strong nationalism can also be observed in the countries of the former Soviet Union, see Chapter 7.

38. Before the SMU, the common silver standard was based on the Hamburg mark.

39. Gourevitch (1977) describes the German example, in which the Prussian junkers, because of their dominant position in German army, judiciary, and bureaucracy were particularly influential. They were able to form a coalition with industrial interests. The determining factor for their rapid success, however, was the assistance provided by the German chancellor Bismarck in

forming the coalition. He did so to raise revenue for the Reich and to build conservative support for his government (Gerschenkron 1943). See also Lambi (1963).

40. This statement, however, has to be qualified for the case of Austro-German Monetary Union which took place *before* German monetary unification and fifteen to twenty years before the change in trade policy. However, the monetary unions of the second half of the nineteenth century, particularly the Latin Monetary Union, were destined to fail from the outset, being initiated in a time of already changing interests.

41. For an overview and critique of hegemonic stability theory, see Haggard and Simmons (1987) and Snidal (1985).

42. Weingast and Marshall (1988) generalize that when agents have private information, moral hazard problems exist and especially when not all contingencies can be specified in advance, "the long arm of future" is not enough to ensure cooperation even in repeated games. Of course this reasoning applies here too.

43. In 1908, however, the actual amount circulating was 16 francs per capita.

44. Another reason might have been the fear of losing admittance to the Paris capital market (Esslen 1917: 131).

45. See Dubois (1950) for a detailed account of the breakdown of the LMU.

46. Although the embargo was effective this time, the Swedish Reiksbank itself later used every opportunity to buy gold coins after it had officially banned them (Bergman et al. 1992) to augment its currency reserves.

4

The Endogeneity of
Fixed Exchange Rates

4.1. Introduction

This chapter starts by offering some evidence on the behavior of flexible exchange rates after the collapse of the Bretton Woods system in 1973. That will be the basis for deriving the position of the tradable and non-tradable goods producing sectors with regard to flexible exchange rates. Some of the arguments resemble those in the preceding chapter but will be treated in more detail here. Moreover, aspects enter which were absent in the nineteenth century. As already indicated in the second chapter, the role of monetary policy has been transformed tremendously during the last century. The recognition of the potentially stabilizing role of monetary policy and the assignment of the task of securing full employment to it went hand in hand with the democratization of society and thus the heightened dependency of governments from widespread public support. The process of "nationalizing" central banks has given governments probably more direction over the monetary process than in the nineteenth century where many central banks were still privately owned. This process has only changed in the recent years in the European Union (EU) and other regions of the world, whereas earlier, disregarding some notable exceptions, most of the central banks have been under the direct control of governments. In this aspect the Keynesian revolution and the output stabilizing role assigned to central banks after the second world war has made this policy change even more forceful since the central banks were directly subject to political influences. The neoclassic revolution and the impotence of monetary policy stressed there, in contrast, had less impact on the political environment than on economic theory. Day to day discussions still assign an output stabilizing role to central banks and monetary policy.

The second major change is the role of money in public finance. Whereas in the nineteenth century money had an important role in the financing of state budgets, especially in the case of wars and other large exogenous shocks it has no longer this role in most developed economies. Some exceptions are countries in the southern tier of the EU, but even there seigniorage revenue is of minor importance relative to the nineteenth century.[1] As the role of money has changed from revenue to output stabilization purposes, also some of the interests with regard to exchange rate flexibility have changed, as this chapter will show.

The chapter proceeds as follows. In the next section, some evidence on the working of flexible exchange rates is reviewed, and the costs and benefits from flexible exchange rates are analyzed from an interest groups' perspective. The following sections use a two-country model to explain the choice and stability of fixed exchange rates, and highlight the recent desire to reach monetary union. On that basis, the stability of an existing monetary union is analyzed. The conclusion applies the results to the European attempt to form a monetary union.

4.2. The Evidence on Flexible Exchange Rates

Contrary to the expectations of proponents of flexible exchange rates (see Friedman 1953), flexible exchange rates have not led to a stabilization of the real exchange rate. While the defenders of flexible exchange rates had expected these to follow relative price changes and thus to ensure a stable real exchange rate, real exchange rates in reality follow movements of nominal exchange rates. The conclusion from this evidence is therefore that the behavior of flexible exchange rates is largely random and unpredictable (Mc Culloch 1983; Mussa 1990). Krugman (1989) even argues that the volatility of real exchange rates has increased by a factor of five since 1973 compared to the periods before.

This has prompted economic theory to shift its focus as well. Attention shifted from trade determined models of exchange rates to portfolio balance models. There is now a consensus that money should be seen as an asset and that exchange rate changes follow the same behavior as other asset prices (Mc Culloch 1983). An exchange rate is the relative price of two fiat moneys, hence of two artificial assets. The supplies and prices of these assets are not natural variables but set by policy (Krugman 1989). And Mussa's verdict about asset markets is very clear:

> I have long been sympathetic to the view that the behavior of asset prices, including exchange rates, is afflicted by some degree of craziness. Many aspects of

human behavior impress me as not entirely sane, and I see no reason why the behavior of asset prices should be a virtually unique exception (1990: 7).

This verdict is obviously addressed to the existence of speculation. There is an argument, based on Nurkse's (1944) description of the interwar years, which maintains that foreign exchange markets are subject to destabilizing speculations. But although destabilizing, this does not mean that such speculation is not rational, as one might conclude from Mussa's statement. Market participants, when expecting a future devaluation, will speculate against a currency and thereby cause the devaluation immediately (Krugman 1979). Obstfeld (1986) shows that indeed expectations can even trigger a rational self-fulfilling crisis, regardless of the underlying fundamentals of the economy. Multiple equilibria are possible which could lead to the collapse of an exchange rate not justified by fundamentals. Expectations of devaluation will lead to speculation against that particular currency and make it thus harder for the authorities to defend their exchange rate. If it becomes impossible for them (for various reasons discussed in Chapter 2), they might give in to speculation and thus make the speculation self-fulfilling. The main problem with adjustable or managed exchange rates under full capital mobility is therefore that speculators try to anticipate changes, thereby provoking occasional speculative attacks on currencies. One suggested solution to this problem has been the introduction of capital controls. I turn to their analysis below.

The Costs of Flexible Exchange Rates

Given that exchange rates swing widely, their instability should influence firms' behavior, and interest groups preferring fixed exchange rates can naturally be found in those sectors exposed to international trade (Eichengreen and Frieden 1993). The reason why this sector prefers fixed exchange rates is that with exchange rate variability foreign trade is exposed to uncertainty in addition to the unavoidable uncertainties created by relative price and aggregate demand variations (Perée and Steinherr 1989). Although it is often argued that short-term risk can easily, albeit not costlessly, be hedged in financial markets, this is much more difficult beyond a one-year period as forward markets are virtually non-existing for periods beyond that period. For if the exchange rate only leads to larger short-term exchange rate movements, the degree of *risk* increases, against which insurance can be bought at a relatively low cost. If instead the floating rate regime leads to long swings in exchange rates, it increases the degree of *uncertainty* (Bernholz 1982). It is generally very difficult to buy insurance against this long-term uncertainty because its pricing is impossible (De Grauwe and de Bellefroid 1989).

It has, hence, frequently been shown theoretically that exchange rate variability decreases the level of activity of a risk-averse internationally exposed firm if hedging is not available (Ethier 1973). The evidence that exchange rate variability is destructive for the level of international trade is, nevertheless, far from being conclusive. On the whole, the majority of studies has failed to find evidence supporting this hypothesis. However, when turning to time-periods longer than one year, the evidence is much stronger that the volume of trade is indeed negatively affected by exchange rate uncertainty (De Grauwe and de Bellefroid 1989; Perée and Steinherr 1989).

While it is debated whether exchange rate changes really lead to reduced international transactions, it is undisputed that currency hedging involves costs. Hedging costs are, however, not the only costs of varying exchange rates. To begin with, Krugman (1989) refers to the widespread pricing to market behavior of international firms. Firms set prices in domestic currencies in that country in which they supply their product. Due to high competition in the foreign market they are forced to fix their prices in the foreign currency and are not able to adjust them according to exchange rate changes. This implies that an exporting firm has to bear the costs of an appreciating home currency and a loss of profits if the exchange rate changes unfavorably.

Moreover, there may be considerable long-term effects involved with exchange rate uncertainty. Dixit (1989) argues that, when future exchange rates are uncertain, there is an incentive for a firm to adopt a wait-and-see attitude towards investment which in turn reduces the rate at which investment adjusts to fundamental factors. If a firms faces costs of entry into and exit from a market, the firm will delay the investment even if appreciation and depreciation are equally likely. This will create a corridor of exchange rate changes in which no adjustments are made by a firm. Exchange rate uncertainty thus leads to too slow an adjustment to changing patterns of comparative advantage. If, however, firms stay in a market although it is temporarily unprofitable, they lose money. There are thus implicit costs of exercising an investment option which have to be added to the visible costs of investment. Consequently, firms invest less which implies opportunity costs and forgone profits.

Likewise, market structures could be influenced by exchange rate variability. Baldwin and Krugman (1989) show that, for large exchange rate changes, a temporary overvaluation is followed by a persistent reduction in the equilibrium exchange rate which is enough to correct the trade balance but not enough to regain once lost markets. For all these reasons it seems likely that industries exposed to exchange rate variability would prefer fixed exchange rates even if they forgo the opportunity to benefit from a devaluating home currency.

A final reason why the exchange regime is more important than a particular level of the exchange rate is that the efficacy of the exchange rate instrument has been considerably reduced in recent years. Increased intra-industrial trade and similarity in production structures in European countries have made the exchange rate an inappropriate and ineffective instrument of adjustment. Exchange rate changes have lost their function as asymmetric shocks became less frequent and important (Gros and Thygesen 1992). Both Germany and France have automotive industries, steel industries and electronic industries, for instance. Since the same industries operate in many European countries, a sector-specific shock will affect these economies in the same way. With shocks to Europe's national economies relatively symmetric in incidence, the costs of abandoning the exchange rate are low (Eichengreen 1993a). I return to this in Chapter 8.

The Benefits of Flexible Exchange Rates

Those for whom cross-border and foreign currency transactions are inconsequential stand to lose the most from fixed parities. For them predictable exchange rates are of little or no value, whereas national reduced autonomy in the formulation of macroeconomic policy may be important.

The possibility of an expansive monetary policy, in contrast, is esteemed because monetary policy can have at least short-run effects on output and employment in the economy. One explanation for this may be sticky nominal wages because of long-term nominal contracts, union monopoly power or price-adjustment costs. Another reason can be found in the literature on coordination failures (see Blanchard 1990, for an overview). If the willingness of an agent to reduce his nominal wage depends on the willingness of others to do so, then a coordination problem arises. That means, no agent is willing to be the first to lower his nominal wage demand. The real wage can nevertheless be brought back in line with prices by inflation and devaluation.[2]

A fixed exchange rate in contrast reduces the flexibility of monetary policy. Imagine a country subjected to a negative shock. If the exchange rate were of no concern, the central bank could initiate expansionary open-market policies to stabilize output. Were it however committed to the maintenance of an exchange rate target, reflation would be impossible because a rapid increase in domestic credit would threaten to produce a loss of international reserves, causing a fatal blow to confidence in exchange rate stability.

Absent the possibility of reflation, other channels of adjustments would be required. The most obvious would be increased wage flexibility. Workers would have to lower their nominal wage demands to provide the necessary real wage flexibility.[3] Therefore, labor would suffer from either unemployment or wage reductions. Another adjustment mechanism would be increased labor mobility between sectors and countries.[4]

The same external constraint limits the use of fiscal policy. By limiting the availability of seigniorage revenue, reduced monetary autonomy influences the range of feasible fiscal policy. Therefore, De Kock and Grilli (1993) identify the need of seigniorage revenue in case of large asymmetric external shocks like wars to be responsible for the collapse of fixed exchange rates. Were a group of countries tied by fixed exchange rates similarly affected by negative shocks, it would be possible to initiate an internationally coordinated monetary expansion in a way that no exchange rate suffered under weakness. In that case, forgoing exchange rate flexibility would incur no costs because the optimal monetary response would be similar for all countries. Only asymmetric shocks require asymmetric responses.

4.3. A Model of Exchange Rate Regime Choice

In this section a model is developed to analyze the distributional conflict between the tradables and the non-tradables sector implied by certain exchange rate regimes and the stability of such a choice, formalizing thus the arguments presented above. In contrast to the standard model in international trade, the Heckscher-Ohlin model, where conflicts arise between factors of production, such as capital and labor, I argue along the lines of a specific-factors model, where both factors of production are immobile in the short-run. The interests of both factors of production are consequently derived along industry lines because factors of production are industry-specific and cannot move across industries instantaneously and without costs. Decreasing output thus results in unemployment and profit loss. Hence, in this model workers and capital owners in a sector have similar interests and unite in their political position.[5]

The model I use here is similar to the one introduced in Chapter 2. It is based on the standard reduced form macroeconomic model developed for monetary and exchange rate policy analysis, where objectives are defined over output and inflation (see e.g. Canzoneri 1985; Cooper 1985; Rogoff 1985a, b). In this chapter the model is extended to incorporate two sectors and two countries. The policymakers in the two countries are concerned with two targets, the rate of change in output because they face an unemployment problem, and the rate of inflation. Each policymaker only disposes of a single policy instrument, the rate of monetary expansion.

The rate of change in output in the tradables sector in the home country

(4.1) $y_T = \gamma\left[m + e\left(1 - \sigma_e^2\right)\right]$

is a positive function of a home component and of net-exports. In this short-run model, an increase in money supply m raises the output of that sector. This positive relationship arises from nominal contracts and adjustment costs which imply that demand management policies can influence output (Blanchard 1990). Moreover, imperfect information about the aggregate price level or from incomplete price adjustments lead to real output effects from money supply increases (see e.g. Romer 1993).[6] The second term, changes in the exchange rate e, defined as the domestic currency price of a unit of foreign currency, captures the change in net-exports. A devaluation makes home-produced goods internationally more competitive and increases exports and output, as long as purchasing power parity is not given. Profits from and production of exports goods, however, are negatively affected by the costs of hedging and by exchange rates variability; σ_e^2 ($0 \le \sigma_e^2 < 1$) captures their adverse influences.[7] It would obviously be higher when exchange rates fluctuate widely. A credible peg, like the EMS during the second half of the 1980s, might lower it in contrast.

The change in output in the non-tradables sector

$$(4.2) \qquad y_N = \gamma m$$

is also positively dependent on money supply increases. For simplification, I exclude any substitutional relation between both goods. This excludes many of the distributional conflicts between the two sectors about the level of exchange rates and allows hence to focus on the exchange rate regime choice.

The exchange rate

$$(4.3) \qquad \frac{e}{\kappa} = m - m^*$$

is given by the difference in rates of money creation in the two countries. This is, of course, a simplification since output effects which also influence the exchange rate are excluded. The parameter κ measures restrictions on capital mobility, where $1 \le \kappa < \infty$. If κ approaches infinity, capital controls ensure that deviations in money supply of the two countries do not affect the exchange rate. $\kappa = 1$ portrays complete capital mobility and the exchange rate reflects instantaneously deviations in money supplies. (The χ from equation 2.3. has been set to one.) κ should be interpreted as a change in the degree of capital restrictions because levels would induce adjustment behavior by agents and lose their effectiveness over time. Wyplosz (1986) argues that capital controls are used in an "on-and-off" fashion, being relaxed in tranquil periods and reinstated when pressures build up on a currency. Like Giovannini (1989), I use capital controls to denote various regulatory manipulations of the market mechanism. These regulations were directed at different markets in different times. Thus, the bond and money markets were unregulated under the gold standard, but not so in the recent Bretton Woods and EMS arrangements. In all three cases, however, central banks resorted to capital controls as an additional instrument of monetary management.[8] Controlling international financial transactions allows a country to gain limited freedom from the "rules of the game" imposed by the domestic and international monetary system by preventing or slowing down the adjustment that would occur if financial transactions were free. They thus provide breathing space, that otherwise would have been absent, to arrange adjustments of monetary policy.

Finally, inflation is given as a function of the rate of money supply increases,

$$(4.4) \qquad\qquad \pi = \phi m \ .$$

Depending on the size of ϕ monetary expansion translates into prices. For a variety of reasons such as menu costs, prices might not adjust fully or with a lag to money supply increases (see Blanchard 1990; Romer 1993).

The last building bloc is the self-interested government's objective function, a political support function. It is given as

$$(4.5) \qquad\qquad V = -\left\{ \left(1-\alpha\right)y_T + \alpha y_N \right\}^2 - \omega\pi^2 \ .$$

The government has a short-time-horizon, wants to be reelected, and is thus interested in maximizing political support.[9] The first term captures the political support the government receives from both sectors by making a policy which helps them to expand their output. α is the political weight the non-tradables sector has which can be interpreted as a function of the size of that sector. Others factors that determine the political influence might be its strategic importance (the military industry) or its symbolic importance (agriculture). Moreover, informal ties might exist between politicians and some sectors. $y_{T,N}$ describes deviations from the target level of employment, i.e., full-employment, in the two sectors, and π deviations of the actual rate of inflation from its target level, assumed to be zero. Inflation is assumed to depend only on the country's own money growth rate which is under the direct control of the government. Money demand shocks and monetary policy control errors are thus excluded. Notice also that the objective function, because of the quadratic formulation, is symmetric for increases and decreases, so deviations from the target in either direction cause disutility. This can be thought of as that optimal levels of employment exist, i.e., full employment, and that unemployment as well as over-employment causes dissatisfaction with the electorate. The same can be said for positive or negative inflation (deflation), because both have redistributional effects which are opposed.

Maximum political support could be hence obtained with full employment and no inflation. All deviations are squared to express increasing marginal dissatisfaction with deviations from the targets. Voters have an increasing aversion to inflation and would thus punish an inflationary government policy. Because both factors of production are, at least in the short run, immobile and mobility entails switching costs, both factor owners prefer to stay in their respective industry. Therefore, factor owners employed in the two industries face a trade-off in their support for monetary expansion and in their inflation aversion. The tradables sector faces, moreover, a trade-off between the positive effects of monetary stimulation and a possible devaluation, while on the other side exchange rate movements affect it negatively via σ_ε^2. (The positive output effect is absent when firms use devaluations not to lower their foreign prices but to increase profits in home currency. This should have a positive employment effect as well which ensures that capital and labor maintain the same interests.) The non-tradables sector only experiences positive output effects from money creation.

The foreign country exhibits the same structural relationships. Foreign variables are marked with an asterisk. The change of output in the foreign tradables sector is

$$(4.6) \qquad y_T^* = \gamma\left[m^* - e\left(1 - \sigma_\varepsilon^2\right)\right],$$

where exchange rate changes exert the opposite effect to that in the home country. Since the exchange rate is the only channel of transmission between the two countries, positive spill-overs from output effects are excluded (for a rich variety of spillover effects, see Canzoneri and Gray 1983). The output of the foreign non-tradables sector is

$$(4.7) \qquad y_N^* = \gamma m^* - \varepsilon^*.$$

To capture the possibility of asymmetric shocks, I introduce a country and sector-specific supply shock ε^* to the foreign country. I focus here only on asymmetric shocks because a common shock on the tradables sector of the two countries could be countered by a common money supply increase. There would be thus no problem for the cooperation between the two countries. Since I am concerned with the viability of cooperation, I only consider asymmetric shocks.

The foreign rate of inflation is given as

$$(4.8) \qquad \pi^* = \phi m^*.$$

For simplicity, I assume that the elasticity of prices with regard to money increases is the same as in the home country.

The foreign government maximizes its political support function

$$(4.9) \qquad V^* = -\left\{(1-\beta)y_T^* + \beta y_N^*\right\}^2 - v\pi^{*2}.$$

Both countries hence differ only in their industry structures, as measured by α and β, the degree of aversion to inflation, and the possibility of an asymmetric shock.

Both governments maximize their respective political support function when setting their monetary policy. This implies as the reaction function for the home country

$$(4.10) \qquad m = \frac{m^*\Delta\Gamma}{\Gamma^2 + \phi^2\omega}$$

with $\Delta \equiv \gamma a\kappa > 0$; $\Gamma \equiv \gamma(1+a\kappa) > 0$; $a \equiv (1-\alpha)(1-\sigma_\epsilon^2) > 0$.

The home country expands its money supply if the foreign country does so to counter negative exchange rate effects which would hurt the tradables sector. This can be interpreted as competitive devaluation. Moreover, the larger the degree of capital controls κ, the more the domestic money supply can be increased to benefit the non-tradables sector without leading to exchange rate movements which are opposed by the tradables sector.

The foreign country's reaction function is

$$(4.11) \qquad m^* = \frac{m\Omega\Psi + \Psi\beta\epsilon^*}{\Psi^2 + \phi^2 v}$$

with $\Omega \equiv \gamma b\kappa > 0$; $\Psi \equiv \gamma(1+b\kappa) > 0$; $b \equiv (1-\beta)(1-\sigma_\epsilon^2) > 0$.

The reaction of the foreign country to the home country's money supply is similar, that is devaluations are countered by expansive monetary policy. In addition, the foreign country will react to the country specific shock ϵ^* by increasing its money supply. Exchange variability and inflation aversion, however, restrict the expansive monetary policy.

The resulting Nash-equilibrium increases in money supplies from (4.10) and (4.11) are

$$(4.12) \qquad m = \frac{\epsilon^*\Psi\beta\Delta\Gamma}{\Theta}$$

and

$$(4.13) \qquad m^* = \frac{\epsilon^* \Psi \beta \left(\Gamma^2 + \phi^2 \omega \right)}{\Theta}$$

with $\Theta \equiv \left(\Gamma^2 + \phi^2 \omega \right)\left(\Psi^2 + \phi^2 v \right) - \Delta \Gamma \Omega \Psi$.

By using the optimal rates of inflation, (4.12) and (4.13) in (4.5) and (4.9), the political support for the two governments is then given as

$$(4.14) \qquad V = -\left\{ -\epsilon^* \frac{\phi^2 \omega \beta \Delta \Psi}{\Theta} \right\}^2 - \omega \left\{ \phi \epsilon^* \frac{\beta \Delta \Gamma \Psi}{\Theta} \right\}^2$$

and

$$(4.15) \qquad V^* = -\left\{ \epsilon^* \beta \Psi \left[\frac{\Psi \left(\Gamma^2 + \phi^2 \omega \right) - \Omega \Delta \Gamma}{\Theta} \right] - \beta \epsilon^* \right\}^2 - v \left\{ \phi \epsilon^* \beta \Psi \frac{\left(\Gamma^2 + \phi^2 \omega \right)}{\Theta} \right\}^2$$

respectively.

4.4. The Stability of Fixed Exchange Rates

Governments are interested in maximizing political support, not only when elections approach but also during their term in office because political support raises funding and donations. It is obvious that the government can benefit its tradables sector by reducing the degree of currency fluctuations, σ_ϵ^2, to zero. By fixing the exchange rate, the output of the tradables sector will increase as described above, since exchange variability decreases that sector's output. Although devaluation could also benefit the tradables sector, risk-averse traders would prefer fixed rates and secure profits as argued above, especially when they have little chances to pass-through the exchange rate changes into prices. Thus, the tradables sector prefers fixed rates and will support such a policy. On the other hand, the non-tradables sector has an incentive to require monetary expansion. Monetary expansion, however, would increase the rate of inflation and hence cost political support. The decisive factor will thus be the relative size of both sectors and the degree of inflation aversion. The larger the tradables sector, the more the government will care for its interests and pursue a policy of fixing exchange rates.

While the sectoral impact of exchange rate regimes helps explain political conflict over this issue, it can explain changes in the support for one or another system over time only if the relative importance and influence of different groups changes. This could be due to changes in the relative size of sectors, their degree of political organisation and the electoral system. If a political system is more responsive to a certain sector, its influence might be more than proportional. Organizational capacities of a sector also affect its political influence. Therefore, one would expect that opening up a country to foreign trade or restructuring the economy towards tradables goods would increase the tradables sector's political influence.[10] As Chapter 3 has shown, the industrial revolution in the nineteenth century and the resulting expansion in international trade caused governments to move towards a policy of monetary integration.

One special reason for the European countries to pursue fixed rates is the Common Agricultural Policy (CAP) of the European Union. A significant change in intra-European exchange rates creates an incentive for producers in the depreciating country to export agricultural products to other member countries. In order to insulate domestic markets from these pressures, intra-European trade in agricultural commodities is supposed to take place at "green exchange rates" which differ from market rates (see Giavazzi and Giovannini 1989). Adjusting these rates, however, becomes increasingly difficult if the nominal rates frequently change. Moreover, the recent reform of the price mechanism in the CAP has caused political pressure in the revaluing countries, like Germany, because farmers are no longer fully compensated for exchange rate losses. Therefore, floating rates constitute a serious obstacle to the survival of the CAP in the common market.

The institutional peculiarity of a fixed exchange rate regime is that one country usually sets the money supply, while the other countries follow by setting the exchange rate. Under the classical gold standard this country was England where the Bank of England acted as the Stackelberg leader for the system. The same role was fulfilled by the U.S. under the Bretton Woods system and by Germany in the EMS. To capture this feature, the home country is assumed to set the rate of money growth in the fixed exchange rate regime m_F while the foreign country stabilizes the exchange rate. Hence the home country is the Stackelberg leader which optimizes by taking into account the reaction function of the foreign country. If the foreign country were the Stackelberg leader, it would set the money supply higher to counter its domestic negative shock. The results would be, however, symmetric in what follows. Only the argumentation for the two countries would be changed.

The political support in the home country for the case of fixed exchange rates is, analogue to (4.5), given by

(4.16) $V_F = -\left\{(1-\alpha)\gamma m_F + \alpha\gamma m_F\right\}^2 - \omega\pi_F^2 .$

The foreign country's support function is, analogue to (4.9),

(4.17) $V_F^* = -\left\{(1-\beta)\gamma m_F + \beta(\gamma m_F - \varepsilon^*)\right\}^2 - \nu\pi_F^{\ 2}$.

In this scenario the Stackelberg leader's choice is to set the money growth rate to zero because it experiences no shock while the foreign country follows domestic monetary policy to keep the exchange rate fixed. Notice that the Stackelberg leader only considers domestic influences when setting his optimal monetary policy in this model because spill-over effects are absent under fixed rates.

The home government prefers the fixed exchange rate regime as long as political support in this regime is higher than under floating rates, hence $V(m) < V_F(m_F)$, where a regime change is assumed to be costless. I thus abstract from exit costs in the form of lost prestige as is often assumed for countries on a fixed rate. Obviously such costs would prolong the survival of a fixed rate regime (see Okzan and Sutherland 1995).

The condition is fulfilled if

(4.18) $(\beta\varepsilon^*)^2\left\{\left(\dfrac{\phi\Psi\Delta}{\Theta}\right)^2\left[\omega\Gamma^2 + (\phi\omega)^2\right]\right\} \geq 0$.

A country does not necessarily prefer being the Stackelberg leader. However, the condition (4.18) is likely to be always fulfilled. The reason for this is very obvious. First, the rate of inflation in the home country is lowered because it can set the optimal money supply without taking the other country into account because the competitive devaluation incentive disappears. The second positive influence stems from the output enhancing role of exchange rate stability in this regime. Thus, the home country can set its preferred rate of monetary expansion without any negative effects from the foreign country's reaction or exchange rate instability. The critical value in that condition is Θ because the larger its size is, the less willing is the home country to accept a fixed exchange rate.

The foreign country chooses fixed exchange rates as long as $V^*(m^*) < V_F^*(m_F^*)$ holds. That is true if

(4.19)
$$\left(\beta\epsilon^{*}\right)^{2}\left\{\left[\frac{\Psi}{\Theta}\left(\Psi\left(\Gamma^{2}+\phi^{2}\omega\right)-\Omega\Delta\Gamma\right)\right]^{2}+v\left[\phi\frac{\Psi}{\Theta}\left(\Gamma^{2}+\phi^{2}\omega\right)\right]^{2}\right.$$
$$\left.-2\frac{\Psi}{\Theta}\left[\Psi\left(\Gamma^{2}+\phi^{2}\omega\right)-\Omega\Delta\Gamma\right]\right\}\geq0.$$

Whether the condition will be fulfilled is again dependent on the size of Θ because it ensures that all terms in equation (4.19) are smaller than one. If it becomes too large, and the external shock on the foreign countries becomes too large, the first two terms, since they square a value smaller than one, may no longer be larger than the linear term.

The fixed exchange rate regime does only survive as long as both conditions (4.18) and (4.19) are simultaneously fulfilled. Hence, countries will support fixed rates as long as asymmetric shocks do not become too large.[11] Whenever (4.19) is no longer fulfilled, the foreign country will abandon a fixed rate regime and return to an independent float. Since a large κ makes diverging money supplies between the two countries compatible with the goal of fixed rates, capital controls support fixed exchange rates to a certain degree (Okzan and Sutherland 1995).[12] This might be the reason why the Bretton Woods system survived for such a long period regardless of divergent inflation performance of the countries involved. Only the massive monetary expansion in the U.S. following the Vietnam war caused its collapse.

Capital controls absent, the setting of monetary policy must be tightly co-ordinated as markets otherwise will test the fixed exchange rate. An example could be seen in the latest EMS crises, see Chapter 6. There, because of the recession in Europe, the EMS partners were no longer willing to follow the tight monetary policy of Germany. They abandoned the exchange rate target, thereby causing the collapse of the EMS.

4.5. The Choice and the Collapse of Monetary Union

This section explains what is special about the European case and why European countries intend to go much further than only fixing their exchange rates, although full monetary union as opposed to a fixed but adjustable exchange rate regime involves abandoning the flexibility of suspending the fixed exchange rate when necessary.

One reason for complete monetary union instead of only fixed rates is certainly that conversion costs can be eliminated. Giovannini (1993c) cites estimates that currency conversion costs average 2.5 percent for travellers and that they fall to 0.05 percent for transactions in excess of $ 5 million.

Averaging across individuals and firms he concludes that conversions costs amount to 0.4 percent of GDP for the EC as a whole. Although no convincing motive for moving towards full monetary union alone, this effect contributes to the gains from monetary union.[13]

The deep reason for monetary union, however, must be seen in the European integration process. Support for EMU increased especially in the 1980s as a result of increasing levels of European trade, reflected by decreases in the α and β terms in the model (see Frenkel and Wei 1993). The increased degree of trade among EU members, especially increased intra-industrial trade, reduced the interests of industries in protection because of the danger of retaliation. This gave rise to the wave for economic integration and finally the Common Market Program (see Schuknecht 1992). The Single European Act of 1986 committed the member countries to reach full mobility of factors of production by 1993.

It is this requirement of full capital mobility which undermined the viability of the EMS in its old form (see also Chapter 2). Periods of fixed exchange rates, accompanied by occasional suspensions as modeled before were possible only because temporary capital controls protected exchange rates and central banks' reserves against speculative attacks (see Wyplosz 1986 for a discussion of temporary capital controls). Firmly fixed exchange rates without the possibility to realign are not credible because it is impossible and undesirable for a political supporting-maximizing government to preclude utilizing the exchange rate instrument. Obstfeld (1994) shows that the existence of an escape clause, as given with adjustable exchange rates, may undermine a government's attempt to defend exchange rates. Therefore, absent the possibility to combine (at least reduced) monetary autonomy with fixed rates, fixed rates are not taken to be irrevocably fixed. Under full capital mobility speculators will test the commitment of central banks and governments to defend the rates and ultimately cause the collapse of the arrangements, as the EMS experience has shown. The only alternative to full monetary union then is a free float. Consequently in the late 1980s and early 1990s the Delors Report and the Maastricht Treaty followed, proposing monetary union.

Hence, under full capital mobility, where $\kappa = 1$, the choice problem for the home country is between monetary union and flexible exchange rates. The political support for monetary union is given by, analogue to (4.5) and (4.9)

(4.20) $$V_U = -\left\{(1-\alpha)\gamma m_U + \alpha\gamma m_U\right\}^2 - \omega\pi_U^2,$$

and

(4.21) $$V_U^* = -\left\{(1-\beta)\gamma m_U + \beta(\gamma m_U - \varepsilon^*)\right\}^2 - \nu\pi_U^2,$$

in the two countries.

The common money supply chosen in the monetary union follows from the joint maximization of the two individual support functions (4.20) and (4.21)

$$(4.22) \qquad m_U = \frac{\gamma\beta\varepsilon^*}{2\gamma^2 + \phi^2(\omega + v)} \equiv \beta\varepsilon^*\eta.$$

Notice that monetary union would imply for the home country that its rate of inflation increases because of joint decision making in the common central bank since $m_U > m_F$. By how much it would increase is dependent on the bargaining power of the countries. For simplification, I assume equal bargaining power.

The assumption is as before that the central bank follows the direction of the governments. This is obviously a simplification since at least the European Central Bank will, according to the Maastricht Treaty, be independent. Thus, the actual money supply set by the European Central Bank might differ from the one derived here.

Political support under monetary union in the two countries is then

$$(4.23) \qquad V_U = -\left\{\gamma\eta\beta\varepsilon^*\right\}^2 - \omega\left\{\phi\eta\beta\varepsilon^*\right\}^2,$$

and

$$(4.24) \qquad V_U^* = -\left\{\gamma\eta\beta\varepsilon^* - \beta\varepsilon^*\right\}^2 - v\left\{\phi\eta\beta\varepsilon^*\right\}^2.$$

Given that monetary union constrains monetary policy in the member countries, the question is for how long it will be viable. Examples for dissolutions of monetary unions can be found in the Latin and the Scandinavian Monetary Unions (Hefeker 1995b), the Austro-Hungarian empire after World War I (Garber and Spencer 1994) and the countries of the ruble zone in the former Soviet Union (Hefeker 1996c) where asymmetric shocks were strong enough to make floating the preferred alternative. Notice, however, that the reasons behind the formation of these currency unions were different to those in the case of the envisaged European monetary union; but political reasons behind monetary unions are exogenous to this model.

The home country supports monetary union as long as $V(m) - S < V_U(m_u)$, where S captures the costs to a country when breaking up a monetary union. These costs can be imagined as the costs of setting up a new central bank, printing new notes and, most importantly, the prestige lost when leaving a monetary union. Moreover, one could imagine that a monetary union treaty involves a penalty for countries breaking their commitment. Although this is only a one time cost, it influences short-term political support and is thus important to the government. For a detailed discussion of switching costs see Dowd and Greenaway (1993).

The home country will fulfill its commitment as long as

$$(4.25) \qquad (\beta\epsilon^*)^2 \left\{ \left(\frac{\phi\Psi\Delta}{\Theta}\right)^2 \left[\omega\Gamma^2 + (\phi\omega)^2\right] - \eta^2(\gamma^2 + \phi^2\omega) \right\} + S \geq 0,$$

while the foreign country demands that $V^*(m^*) - S < V_U^*(m_u^*)$, where switching costs are assumed to be equal for the two countries. That is given if

$$(4.26)$$
$$(\beta\epsilon^*)^2 \left\{ \left[\left(\frac{\Psi}{\Theta}(\Psi(\Gamma^2 + \phi^2\omega) - \Omega\Delta\Gamma)\right)^2 - (\gamma\eta)^2 \right] + v\phi^2 \left[\left(\frac{\Psi}{\Theta}(\Gamma^2 + \phi^2\omega)\right)^2 - (\gamma\eta)^2 \right] \right.$$
$$\left. -2\left[\left(\frac{\Psi}{\Theta}(\Psi(\Gamma^2 + \phi^2\omega) - \Omega\Delta\Gamma)\right) - \gamma\eta \right] \right\} + S \geq 0.$$

Both conditions are similar to (4.18) and (4.19). Only $\gamma\eta$ and $\eta^2(\gamma^2 + \phi^2\omega)$ are subtracted respectively. But that influence is small since η ensures that those terms are smaller than one. For the home country this influence is negative because it implies that the common money supply increase reacts to the foreign shock. This unambiguously increases the rate of inflation for the home country. For the foreign country this effect is ambiguous because the potential money supply increases to counter the shock also raise the rate of inflation. The size of switching costs S, moreover, is very important in the decision whether to abandon the monetary union. Hence the establishment of a common central bank and the introduction of one physical monetary system will unambiguously prolong the survival of a monetary union. Switching costs can therefore compensate for the abolition of capital controls whose absence make the conditions harder to fulfill.

4.6. Conclusion

The model developed in this chapter is used to analyze cycles in the choice of exchange rate regimes across time and countries. It is shown that sectoral shifts, especially the enlargement of the tradables sector, implies a change in the political equilibrium in a country towards fixed exchange rates. Because the tradables sector suffers from floating rates it will prefer fixed rates. The occurrence of asymmetric shocks, however, will induce a political support-maximizing government to increase the money supply. If shocks are large enough and asymmetrically distributed, political equilibria will shift towards floating rates because fixed rates are incompatible with monetary autonomy.

Institutional changes in the economic environment, especially the abolition of capital controls, make fixed but adjustable rates no longer viable. Hence, the choice for a government shifts to that between floating rates and full monetary union. This particularly explains the desire to reach full monetary union in Europe. In this logic monetary union will inevitably follow and its survival will depend on the costs of abandoning that regime and, most importantly, on the occurrence and nature of asymmetric shocks. Increased similarity and trade among the European economies will, however, increase the viability of that arrangement. Large tradables sectors will push for monetary integration and since they are similarly affected by shocks, there is no reason for a government to break up the arrangement because a concerted action to help those sectors is possible. Only when the size of α and β is too far apart conflicts will arise. Less support for EMU could probably be expected from large countries with a larger non-tradables sector.

The question about the distribution of shocks in an EMU is finally an empirical one. Asymmetric shocks, or the expectation of such shocks, like oil-price shocks for the U.K., should seriously undermine support for EMU in those countries as well. Studies looking into the likelihood of asymmetric shocks come to opposing results depending on the development of the production structures in EMU. On the one hand it is argued that integration in Europe will lead to increased intra-industrial trade because of economies-of-scale (European Commission 1990). This structure of trade leads, of course, to similar shocks across countries in the future. As far as countries produce similar products, they will be affected similarly by shocks. The other side of the integration coin is another dynamic effect. Krugman (1991) has argued that trade integration which occurs as a result of economies-of-scale also leads to a regional concentration of industrial activities. Thus two effects from integration are possible. It can either lead to a production closer to the market or to a regional concentration, which exploits static and dynamic economies-of-scale, with different implication for the future probability of asymmetric shocks and the necessity of asymmetric policy responses.[14]

Notes

1. This is of course also a major critique to the seigniorage determined approach to optimum currency areas as in Canzoneri and Gray (1990). For most of the European economies this approach is irrelevant because seigniorage revenue is negligible (see also Cohen and Wyplosz 1989).

2. This is Friedman's (1953) "daylight savings time" argument.

3. Horn and Persson (1988) show theoretically that fixed exchange rates can lead to more wage flexibility. Epstein (1991) concludes thus that capital owners prefer fixed exchange rates. Alogoskoufis and Smith (1989) show that wage setting behavior is indeed influenced by the exchange rate regime.

4. This is Mundell's (1961) classic criterion for optimum currency areas. Blanchard and Katz (1992) show for the U.S. that most regional adjustment between depressed and prospering regions is provided by labor movements instead of wage adjustments. For the European Union, however, the degree of labor mobility is much smaller, hence wage flexibility would have to substitute for labor mobility in Europe.

5. Fixed nominal exchange rate might lead to real exchange variability. Real exchange rate variability, of course, implies that the non-tradables sector suffers since non-tradables prices have to adjust to bring back the real exchange rate to its original level. But it is well-known that real exchange variability is closely connected to nominal exchange rate variability (see Section 4.2). Non-tradables price adjustment to ensure a constant real exchange rate is thus not guaranteed. Likewise, fixing exchange rates between countries at misaligned rates implies redistribution between them. For example, it is a widely held view that Germany's export sector benefited from the EMS because it lead to real overvaluation in higher inflation countries like France or Italy. These effects are disregarded here as well.

6. The assumption is that monetary policy is the only instrument the government can use. This could be explained by the slow working of fiscal expenditures or some balanced budget requirement. Would budget expenditures be financed by seigniorage (as in De Kock and Grilli 1993) the model could also be applied.

7. If firms exhibit pricing to markets behavior as might be possible (see Section 4.2.), the positive effect from a devaluation is lost. Instead, only the negative effect from variability σ_e^2 would be given. This would strengthen firms' interest for fixed exchange rates. Obviously, the quantitative effect of σ_e^2 might differ considerable depending on the products concerned.

8. Under the gold standard bonds and money were left unregulated. Nevertheless, the textbook example of unrestricted working of the Humean "price specie flow mechanism" does not adequately describe the situation. Central banks often suspended "the rules of the game" by manipulating the gold points, that is the bid-ask spread on bullion charged by the central bank. Moreover, central banks changed discount rates to influence gold flows (see Bloomfield 1959; Viner 1932).

9. This formulation only allows for one kind of influence on political decision making. It does not capture lobbying expenditures or corruption. The government does not "sell" policies and the sectors "play fair" in the sense that they only offer votes, but not money. Moreover, any direct foreign influence on domestic decisions is ruled out. This is, of course, a simplification, as detailed in Chapter 2.

10. Note that this corresponds to Mc Kinnon's (1963) optimum currency area criterion.

11. Cases where realignments of fixed rates suffice are not modeled. One justification for this might be that large shocks are followed by continued monetary expansion. Eichengreen (1992) for instance shows that a fiscal war of attrition followed World War I which forced governments to continue money creation instead of tax-financing the budget.

12. Gros (1992), however, argues that it is less due to capital controls than to the willingness of governments to defend their exchange rate target that the EMS survived for such a long period.

13. As these costs constitute to a large extent profits for the financial industry, Giovannini (1993c) concludes that this industry tends to lose from monetary union. Others identify this industry as behind the movement towards monetary union (Eichengreen and Frieden 1993). Grüner and Hefeker (1996) offer a solution to this apparent paradox. See Chapter 5 for details.

14. For a summary of this discussion, see De Grauwe (1994).

5

Industrial Interests in Monetary Union: The Banking Industry

5.1. Introduction

Fixing exchange rates eliminates their variability, and that is what enterprises that are internationally active look for. This is the argument of the preceding chapter. The support of those enterprises for monetary union, it was argued, is based on the unsustainability of fixed exchange rates under full capital mobility. This chapter qualifies that argument. First, I briefly review some arguments made in the literature about the additional effects of a common currency that go beyond the benefits from stable currency relations. The main part of this chapter will then develop the difference between large and small industry in the tradable goods sector. The analysis focuses on the banking industry because it is striking how determined part of this industry pursues monetary union (see Hefeker 1996b, for details). One possible explanation for this could be its tight links to large industry. As Henning (1994) argues, banks that have tight institutionalized links with enterprises are likely to pursue those industries' aims as well for the obvious reasons that their own well-being and profits are closely connected to that of the industry. If major industry profits from monetary union, for the reasons laid out in the preceding chapter, than banks will adopt the same strategy. On the other hand, it is remarkable that major banks in European countries are much more determined in their support for EMU than major enterprises are, at least if one judges from the public statements made by them. One thus gets the impression that major banks might have an additional reason to push for monetary union. This additional reason is explored in this chapter. The focus is on the German example because German private banks are particularly vigorous in their pursuit of EMU.

As indicated above, the argument about the distributional implications of EMU for large and small enterprises is not restricted to the banking industry.

Most of the influences can be seen in other tradable industries as well. But for the banking industry, EMU has an additional effect which is probably less important in other industries. That is, the amount of common regulation for the entire industry going hand in hand with EMU. That common regulation and setting of European wide standards for other industries has come already with the Common Market Program. Only for the banking industry, one could expect another influential effect in this regard with the movement to a common central bank.

This chapter thus derives distributional effects of monetary union by focusing on the effects of changes in banking policy which necessarily accompany monetary and financial integration. While monetary policy is the action taken by a central bank to achieve objectives in terms of price level stability, employment and interest rates, banking policy focuses on actions *vis-à-vis* commercial banks or other financial institutions, together with financial regulation and banking supervision (see Giovannini 1993b). Building on this distinction, the chapter explores the role and interests of large commercial banks in the process of monetary integration. Starting out with the common market project, it is argued that large commercial banks are not only interested in full financial integration but also gain from a single currency and unification of banking regulation. While the first point is rather obvious and has been frequently observed in the literature (see e.g. Cohen 1989), the second seems at first glance rather paradoxical because banks profit from currency transactions. Giovannini (1993c) hence views the transactions costs savings through monetary union as a distribution of resources between the financial and nonfinancial sector. In Giovannini's estimation these amount to 4 to 5 percent of total value added in the EU financial sector and he consequently identifies "a significant transfer of resources across two clearly identifiable interest groups: from international banks to their clients involved in cross-border transactions within Europe" (Giovannini 1993c: 16). Nevertheless, public wisdom broadly views the common market and monetary integration projects as being driven by the large industry and business leaders who try to exploit economies of scale (Casella 1992a). This view is justified by explicit statements by major European banks in favor of monetary union (see Frieden 1991; Lipp et al. 1992; and Weber 1993).

The chapter offers a solution to this seeming paradox between the fact that, on the one hand, public discussion assumes the financial industry and major banks to be behind the European integration process and, on the other hand, that the banking industry loses profits when a common currency is introduced. While banks clearly lose some profits in form of the margins they take when converting currencies, much larger gains can be identified arising from monetary union implying common regulation of the European banking industry through a common central bank and, specifically, increased cooperation among European banks.

But the resulting effects for banks are not at all unambiguous. It turns out that only the large banks will gain from cooperation across borders because of their larger *national* market share for international transactions.[1] There is hence a conflict between large and small banks in their position concerning EMU. Only large banks can afford the costs arising from cooperation across borders because of their size. Therefore differences in size and reduction in variable costs by cooperation determine the position of a particular bank with regard to EMU. Even a uniform reduction of transaction costs for cooperating and non-cooperating banks due to the fact that exchange transactions are no longer necessary affects market structure and thus large banks' profits.

The chapter proceeds as follows. First, I briefly review the arguments for a common currency that go beyond the effects derived in the last chapter. The next section gives a broad overview of the structure of the market for banking services in major European countries, the cross-border cooperation among European banks, and the position of banks concerning EMU. I then flesh out the argumentation in full and develop a model to highlight the effects of monetary union on the European banking market.

5.2. Benefits from a Common Currency

The most obvious reason for expecting significant economic gains from a common currency is through the abolition of all exchange rate related transaction costs. These direct effects have been estimated by the European Commission (1990) by calculating the sum of all transaction costs that arise in intra-community transactions. The direct savings in transaction costs should therefore be around one fourth to one half of one percent of the GDP of the Union. Gros and Thygesen (1992) estimate total annual transaction costs savings between 13.0 and 17.9 billion ECU from a common currency.

It has been argued that the effects of the savings of transaction costs are of the same order of magnitude as the abolition of border controls under the common market program. Further beneficial effects can be expected through the elimination of information costs and price discrimination (Gros and Thygesen 1992). Thus the gains are estimated to be as large as those calculated by the Checchini-Report, and hence the overall GDP in the Union could raise by as much as 4.5-6.5 percent.

Finally, Baldwin (1991) has argued that dynamic effects could be expected from a common currency. The increase in overall efficiency that comes through the common currency translates into an increase of the marginal productivity of capital. This should lead to higher investment and to a higher capital stock, leading to more output with the same labor force.[2] The multiplier estimated by

Baldwin of the output effect from induced capital formation is two. Moreover, the Commission's (European Commission 1990) study about the common currency has argued that reduced uncertainty from a common currency leads to more investment across borders. Most of these effects, however, it has been argued accrue to large enterprises instead of small ones because economies-of-scale are involved, or small enterprises are more risk-averse and thus not willing to use the enlarged opportunities.

5.3. Liberalization and Concentration in the European Banking Market

When taking a first look at the banking market in major European countries, the most striking impression is the high degree of concentration (see Canals 1993, and Grüner and Hefeker 1996). While few large banks generally have an almost dominant market share, the rest is divided among a much larger number of small banks. Therefore, it is important to take this dichotomy into account when analyzing the European banking market and the actions taken by banks and their position *vis-à-vis* monetary union and financial liberalization.

The second feature of the European banking market is the process of liberalization in financial services. In 1985 the member countries of the EC adopted the Single European Act, aiming for a completion of the "Common Market" in 1992. In late 1986, this was followed by a formal agreement to remove controls on a wide variety of capital movements within the community. The process of liberalization and deregulation, however, began much earlier, albeit without full liberalization of capital movements. In 1977 the First Banking Directive of the EC, applying to all banking institutions, made the first step toward harmonizing supervision and regulation for these institutions. This directive required member countries to introduce a common system for authorization of new banks based on a minimum amount of capital and an honest, experienced management. In practice, however, member countries possessed much tighter national regulations. The Second Banking Directive, adopted in 1988 by the Council of Ministers, is based on the Single Market Program of 1985 which laid down the principle of "mutual recognition" for the unification of financial markets. Finally, in June 1989 the Single Banking Licence was created. It permits any bank to establish and to offer a broad range of financial services in any other member country on the basis of only one licence issued by the home country (Canals 1993).

The effect of deregulation and liberalization is necessarily a higher degree of competition among banks, or this one would at least suppose. The reaction of banks naturally is action to prevent too much competition. They react to the increase in competition by trying to reduce their rivalry via mergers, acquisitions and cross-participation agreements (Canals 1993).[3] One potential reason for doing so is that, if there was collusion among banks, it would be easier to sustain with fewer rivals and that margins are larger under cooperation. Another reason is, of course, the realization of economies-of-scale and -scope (Vives 1991). An increase in the number of branches gives rise to network externalities because for the consumer this is an important consideration when choosing his or her financial institution. This also constitutes an important barrier to entry because it gives rise to economies-of-scale.

Against this background of concentration, cooperation and financial liberalization, one has to analyze the interests of the banks. Why do banks support financial liberalization and monetary integration given the implied increase of competition? One possible answer to this question would build on the consensus in the theoretical literature that capital owners and financial institutions gain from the common market program. Frieden (1991) states that financial integration and liberalization of capital movements tend to benefit owners of mobile capital and diversified assets because investment opportunities are increased. Furthermore the number of transactions will increase. That is why Europe's leading financial and multinational firms have been the stronghold of support for breaking down remaining barriers to EU financial and monetary integration. Cohen (1989) in contrast makes a clear distinction between the larger banks and the smaller ones in their interest for financial integration in Europe. High concentration and the fact that only the larger banks are already involved in international banking business gives rise to an important cleavage. Europe's large banks already earn a sizable portion of their profits from cross-border operations. Hence, they are probably seeing a single market rather as an opportunity than as a threat. In contrast, the small banks are probably benefiting from national regulation and restriction on rights of establishment and operation.

The evidence, however, is that major banks not only favor financial integration but lobby for the movement to full monetary union. For example, in Britain's Association for Monetary Union in Europe, a private-sector lobbying organization for rapid currency union, eight of the twelve firms organized in this group are firms in the financial and related services sector, among which are Barclays and Citibank.[4] Likewise, the three largest German banks, in a statement of their chief-economists, vigorously defended the project of monetary union against the caveats of more than 60 German economists (see Lipp et al. 1991). More recently they also welcomed the "green book" about the realization of EMU prepared by the Commission, which met skepticism by central bankers and politicians (see Hefeker 1996b). In contrast, small banks are reluctant towards the idea of monetary union in the foreseeable future (see e.g., the annual reports of the BVR 1987-1993). Why, then, is financial liberalization obviously not enough for major European banks? Why do they favor fixed exchange rates, and why do they even go further and demand monetary union while small banks oppose it?

The first rough impression is that those who suffer most from currency volatility stand to gain the most from monetary union. These include major banks and corporations with pan-EC investment or trade interests (Eichengreen and Frieden 1993). On the other hand, the European Commission (1990) has carried out an assessment of the magnitude of transaction costs incurred by European countries because of the existence of various currencies. It estimates ECU 6.2 to 10.4 billion (June 1990) for turnover in the foreign exchange market multiplied by bid-ask spreads in the foreign exchange markets, netting out transactions in the interbank market and transactions involving nonmember currencies. Adding costs in the retail foreign exchange market and the costs of cross-border payments, treasury measurement in companies running separate wholesale payments systems across Europe adds to a total cost of 13.1 and 19.2 billion ECU for the EU countries. The costs amount to 4 to 5 percent of the total value added in the EU financial sector, where the largest part of it goes through London. Since this constitutes a transfer of resources between the financial and the nonfinancial sectors, Giovannini (1993c) concludes that the creation of a single currency represents a significant redistribution of resources between two clearly identifiable interest groups. Based on the so-called transaction costs model, he predicts that international banks should resist the adoption of a single currency, in order to avoid the costs of adjusting to a new business environment, while firms which are involved in cross-border trade within the EU should favor it.

One possible reason why large banks nevertheless lobby for monetary union is that monetary union can be seen as a commitment to the common market and financial liberalization. Without monetary union, given fixed exchange rates, there is an obvious danger that governments resort to capital controls to defend the exchange rate band (Eichengreen 1993a). From this perspective, monetary union is the logical and only permissible solution to secure the common market for capital and services. It is thus an integral part of the common market and as such in the interest of large firms and banks.

The next section, however, offers an alternative solution to the above puzzle by explicitly taking into account the structure of the banking market in Europe. The high degree of concentration gives rise to a cleavage between large and small banks because the competition for market shares is one reason why large banks prefer a single European market. Monetary integration, moreover, and the implied common regulation of the banking business reduce variable costs for cross-border transactions. The following section analyzes the effects of a cost reduction on market structure and profits in the concentrated oligopolistic market for transborder financial services.

5.4. Large Banks, Small Banks, and the Effects of EMU

The Domestic Market

In this section a simple model of the oligopolistic market for cross-border banking services in Europe is developed. The attention is restricted to transactions which involve cross-border capital movements and abstracts from the domestic market, that is transactions between regions within one country. The setting is an imperfect competition framework, where only two banks, a large bank (indexed i) and a small bank (indexed j), find themselves in Cournot competition. Moreover, only the domestic market is modeled, that is I only look at the choices domestic banks face concerning international cooperation. Both banks have the same general profit function.

The profit function of a large bank is given by:

$$(5.1) \qquad \Pi_i = px_i - x_ic_i - \xi_iF, \quad \xi_i = \begin{cases} 0, \text{ no cooperation} \\ 1, \quad \text{cooperation} \end{cases}$$

where p is the market price for the transaction, x_i the quantity supplied and c_i measures marginal costs. F is a fixed cost parameter to measure the one-time costs of setting up a cooperation among banks in Europe. The marginal costs c_i are assumed to depend on three variables: the size of the bank s_i, the cooperation dummy ξ_i and the monetary and financial regime R

$$(5.2) \qquad c_i = c(s_i, \xi_i, R).$$

s_i measures the relative advantages the large bank has. It can be thought of as the size of the subsidiaries network of the bank, giving rise to network externalities or as economies-of-scale and -scope which characterize the banking market. The larger the number of subsidiaries the bank has, the lower are its costs of doing business internationally. The second assumption is that there are cost economies in international bank transactions. If banks cooperate internationally, they can reduce their variable costs by Δv. c is assumed to fall if banks cooperate internationally because cooperation reduces the costs of transborder transactions for any single bank. While, on the one hand, cooperation implies considerable fixed costs of doing so, not only when buying a foreign bank but also when building new departments to deal with the foreign partner, to exchange personnel and so on, it, on the other hand, reduces variable costs. A reduction of variable costs arises because now there is an established net of contacts for every cross-border business, on-line computer connections, and the like. Apart from these technical details, established contacts and frequent meetings build trust among business partners and might also lead to faster and less costly dealings.

Finally the monetary and fiscal regime matters. The variable costs are reduced when banks are subject to common regulation in all places in which they conduct business and if exchange transactions are abandoned in the case of monetary union. This means that similar reserve requirements and supervision in all of Europe lower costs of doing business for international banks. Marginal costs are not affected by financial liberalization however.

This leads to the following specification for marginal costs:

$$(5.3) \qquad c_i = c(s_i, \xi_i, R) = \overline{v} - r(R) - \xi_i \Delta v + f(s_i) \ ,$$

where $\overline{v}$ is a given threshold level of marginal costs in absence of financial liberalization and monetary union. r is a reduction of marginal costs compared to this reference situation, and it captures the reduction of transaction costs that arises from abandoning exchange transactions that would otherwise be necessary in international transactions. The function f, which captures size differences among banks, is assumed to be strictly decreasing and set to $f(s) = 1/s$.

Finally the threshold level of marginal cost for a given regime R as $v^N(R) = \overline{v} - r(R)$ is defined. Thus v^N is the level of marginal costs when all size economies are exhausted and when there is no international cooperation. Given what has been said before v^N (MU) < v^N (no MU, FL) = v^N (no MU, no FL) where MU and FL stand for monetary union and financial liberalization respectively. This yields for marginal costs:

$$(5.4) \qquad c_i = c(s_i, \xi_i, R) = v^N(R) - \xi_i \Delta v + \frac{1}{s_i} \ .$$

Given the imperfect competition structure in the domestic banking markets, both large and small banks have to decide whether they should cooperate with partner banks in the respective European country, merge with them or acquire a foreign bank. The decisions are assumed to be made simultaneously in stage one of the game.

The price charged for cross-border financial services is defined via a standard inverse demand function

$$(5.5) \qquad p = a - bX \ ,$$

where a can be interpreted as the size of the domestic market for international banking services. I assume that national demand is always addressed to domestic banks, whether they cooperate internationally or not. $X = x_i + x_j$ is the total amount of financial services supplied by all banks, x_i and x_j being the supply of the large and the small bank respectively. A cooperating bank is assumed to obtain the gains arising from its domestic business. Thus I abstract from issues of negotiations and distribution of aggregated profits in different countries among cooperating banks.

The Cournot equilibrium of the game, given marginal costs, is described by the quantities

$$(5.6) \qquad x_i = \frac{1}{3b}\left(a + c_j - 2c_i\right),$$

and

$$(5.6') \qquad x_j = \frac{1}{3b}\left(a + c_i - 2c_j\right).$$

The national equilibrium is given by the following total supply (the sum of x_i and x_j)

$$(5.7) \qquad X = \frac{2}{3}\frac{a}{b} - \frac{1}{3b}\left(c_i + c_j\right),$$

where the market clearing price of services is given by

$$(5.8) \qquad p = \frac{1}{3}a + \frac{1}{3}\left(c_i + c_j\right).$$

Profits for the individual bank are hence given as

$$(5.9) \qquad \Pi_i = \frac{1}{9b}\left(a + c_j - 2c_i\right)^2 - \xi_i F$$

and

$$(5.9') \qquad \Pi_j = \frac{1}{9b}\left(a + c_i - 2c_j\right)^2 - \xi_j F$$

respectively. It is obvious from equations (5.9) and (5.9') that the fixed costs F influence both banks similarly, while the relative and absolute size of a bank has an important influence on the equilibrium decision.[5]

The Effects of "Europe 1992"

The effects of different institutional arrangements on the market structure and on each bank's profits are analyzed next. The single market and economic integration are usually expected to expand the cross-border trade in Europe. According to the famous Cecchini Report, increased intra-industrial trade and economies-of-scale should contribute to a larger volume of trade, accompanied by increased direct investment and portfolio investment (see also European Commission 1990, and Baldwin 1991). Increased cross-border transactions will, of course, also entail expanded business for banks because transborder payments increase. This corresponds to an increase of the parameter a in the model. Effects on the threshold level of variable costs v^N are, however, unlikely to appear.

European Monetary Union and Banking Policy

Since it is clear that a monetary union must comprise a *common* and *single* central bank, the nature of the banking business is transformed. A single central bank must necessarily unify regulations and supervision for the whole of its territory (Giovannini 1993b). Under the Second Banking Directive, which follows the principle of mutual recognition, no substitution of national regulation is required unless necessary. While home-countries are in charge of supervision, host countries' authorities are in charge of liquidity ratios. However, the EU member countries are supposed to make necessary changes in their national laws to conform to the EC directives. Therefore, be it either because of the harmonized rules of the single-market directives, or as a result of competitive deregulation due to the freedom of establishment in the banking industry, bank regulations will become approximately homogeneous across member countries. To the extent that activities of financial firms go beyond their national borders, there is a clear reason to encourage tight cooperation among national authorities. Because the linkage of national payments systems will inevitably give rise to arbitrage-induced payments-routing, one could expect the substitution of national systems with a new, EU-wide wholesale payments system managed by the common central bank. Thus, problems of payments systems suggest a negative answer to the question of whether the presence of a variety of financial systems and institutions is compatible with a single currency (Giovannini 1993b).

Given this requirement of common regulation, one could expect a uniform reduction in the variable costs of cross-border transactions, expressed as a reduction of marginal costs in the model. Not only is there certainly a reduction in the fixed costs from adapting to different regulations in different countries, but accounting procedures will be unified as well. Furthermore, exchange transactions are no longer necessary.

5.5. Distributional Effects of Monetary Union

Now explicit propositions about when one will see international cooperation among large banks and no cooperation among small banks can be derived. Those will allow to explain the stylized facts presented above and establish the interests of large banks in monetary union.

In the first condition, marginal-cost structures that will lead to asymmetric international cooperation are derived. In the second condition, the necessities for symmetric equilibria where both the large and the small bank do or do not cooperate are derived. Both conditions explain why decreasing marginal costs for both the cooperating and the non-cooperating bank can induce a change in the market structure. [6]

Asymmetric Cooperation

The condition for the case where only the large bank cooperates is that the large bank gains from cooperation when the small bank does not cooperate, while the small bank does not cooperate when the large bank does.

The first condition, that is the large bank gains, by using (5.3) in (5.9) can be written

$$(5.10) \quad \frac{1}{9b}\left[a+\left(v^N+\frac{1}{s_j}\right)-2\left(v^N+\frac{1}{s_i}-\Delta v\right)\right]^2 - F >$$
$$\frac{1}{9b}\left[a+\left(v^N+\frac{1}{s_j}\right)-2\left(v^N+\frac{1}{s_i}\right)\right]^2,$$

while the small bank does not cooperate iff

$$(5.11) \quad \frac{1}{9b}\left[a+\left(v^N+\frac{1}{s_i}-\Delta v\right)-2\left(v^N+\frac{1}{s_j}-\Delta v\right)\right]^2 - F <$$
$$\frac{1}{9b}\left[a+\left(v^N+\frac{1}{s_i}-\Delta v\right)-2\left(v^N+\frac{1}{s_j}\right)\right]^2.$$

Both conditions can be rewritten respectively as

(5.10')
$$\Delta v^2 > \frac{9}{4}bF - \Delta v\left(a + \frac{1}{s_j} - \frac{2}{s_i} - v^N\right)$$

and

(5.11')
$$\Delta v\left(a + \frac{1}{s_i} - \frac{2}{s_j} - v^N\right) < \frac{9}{4}bF .$$

It is obvious that non-cooperation of both the large and the small bank results if the cost reduction due to cooperation is relatively small. This leads to the condition for symmetric behavior by both banks.

Symmetric Cooperation and Non-Cooperation

The conditions for a non-cooperative Nash-equilibrium are easily derived from what has been said before. To derive the case of non-cooperation of the large banks, (5.10'), the condition for the cooperation of the large bank, changes the sign

(5.12)
$$\Delta v^2 < \frac{9}{4}bF - \Delta v\left(a + \frac{1}{s_j} - \frac{2}{s_i} - v^N\right) .$$

Likewise, the condition for the non-cooperation of the small bank is obtained by exchanging indices

(5.12')
$$\Delta v^2 < \frac{9}{4}bF - \Delta v\left(a + \frac{1}{s_i} - \frac{2}{s_j} - v^N\right) .$$

Finally, to derive the condition for the cooperation of the small bank, one simply reverses the sign for inequality in (5.11')

(5.13)
$$\Delta v\left(a + \frac{1}{s_i} - \frac{2}{s_j} - v^N\right) > \frac{9}{4}bF .$$

The condition for cooperation of the large bank is again obtained by exchanging indices

(5.13')
$$\Delta v \left(a + \frac{1}{s_j} - \frac{2}{s_i} - v^N \right) > \frac{9}{4} bF .$$

A Change in the Equilibrium

The analysis so far established conditions for asymmetric cooperation and symmetric cooperation and noncooperation. How can the step towards monetary union lead from the latter equilibrium to the former one? The introduction of monetary union is characterized by a reduction of variable costs for cooperating and non-cooperating banks due to the fact that currency exchange operations become unnecessary. I assume here that the reduction has the same size for both types of banks . The consequence of such a reduction in marginal costs can be seen in Figure 5.1.

FIGURE 5.1. The intervals of asymmetric cooperation before (AC) and after (AC') monetary union.

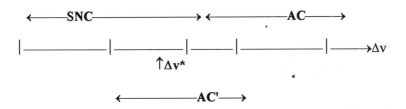

The interval SNC is the interval of symmetric non-cooperation in the initial situation of no monetary union derived as the second step. AC is the interval of asymmetric cooperation derived before. Now suppose that before monetary union cooperation does not pay for the large enterprise. In this case Δv must lie in SNC, for example Δv^*. The entry into monetary union leads to a reduction of v^N. The interval for asymmetric cooperation thus moves to the left and becomes AC'. The intersection of AC' and SNC is the interval for Δv which is associated with a change in the market structure for a given reduction of v^N. Note that from the condition set above an asymmetric cost reduction, that is an increase of Δv, would additionally increase the chances for a change in the market structure.

Given the before- and after-EMU cost differential Δv^*, the move to EMU induces a change in the market structure if the size of the cost reduction for cooperating and noncooperating players is sufficiently large to move the new interval of asymmetric cooperation, AC', sufficiently far to the left.

Asymmetric Effects of Monetary Union

As the last step it can be shown that the large bank always gains from monetary union. The small bank only gains, however, if the type of equilibrium does not change. If the type of equilibrium changes to asymmetric cooperation, the effect of monetary union on the profits of the small bank is negative if Δv is sufficiently large.

This can be seen by considering the profit function (5.9) before monetary union when both banks do not cooperate. Joint reduction of variable costs makes monetary union more attractive for both players if they do not cooperate. Asymmetric cooperation additionally benefits the large bank if (5.11') is fulfilled. Profits in this new equilibrium for the small bank are smaller than before:

(5.14)

$$\frac{1}{9b}\left[a+\left(v_{MU}^N+\frac{1}{s_i}-\Delta v\right)-2\left(v_{MU}^N+\frac{1}{s_j}\right)\right]^2 < \frac{1}{9b}\left[a+\left(v^N+\frac{1}{s_i}\right)-2\left(v^N+\frac{1}{s_j}\right)\right]^2.$$

The small bank loses from monetary union if Δv, the cost reduction for the large bank from cooperation, exceeds $r = v^N - v_{MU}^N$, the cost reduction due to monetary union.

Earlier I have derived that monetary union will induce a simultaneous decrease in variable costs for both large and small banks. The third condition establishes the main result that such a symmetric reduction of variable costs can induce a change in the market structure with asymmetric effects on profits of small and large banks. Note also that an increasing market size, a, following from the common market, also moves the interval of asymmetric cooperation to the left and thereby triggers a change in the market share to the benefit of large banks. This result is able to explain the paradox that large banks favor monetary union despite forgoing profits from exchange transactions. Perfectly in line with this result, one observes that large banks build cross-border strategic alliances. This explains why large banks favor a rapid movement to monetary union and are particularly in favor of the rigid time table of the Maastricht Treaty.

5.6. Conclusion

This chapter has explained why large banks favor European Monetary Union although high mark-ups on international financial transactions will be reduced. The solution to this puzzle is based on the observation that the market structure for bank transactions is currently dominated by a number of large national banks which compete with smaller regional ones. Assuming that monetary union will change the variable costs for both cooperating and non-cooperating banks, I have argued that this effect could bring together the critical mass necessary to induce changes in the market structure so that the demand for international transactions will almost exclusively be served by the large cooperating banks. There are at least two reasons to assume lower variable costs with monetary union: one is the fact that transaction costs for exchange operations vanish. The second point is that the unification of bank regulation laws will reduce the marginal costs for cross-border transactions again. The model, thus, predicts a deepening of existing international cooperations of large banks and a dramatic change in the market structure for international transactions occurring with monetary union.

The question is of course in how far the argumentation of this chapter can be extended to other industries than the banking industry. It should be applicable to other industries where economies-of-scale and international cooperation matter. And as the list in Footnote 4 shows, there are more industries behind monetary union than just the financial industry. Moreover, all of these are major enterprises, but only the small banking industry is explicit in its reluctance concerning early EMU. Interestingly, many small enterprises in other industries obviously think they are not affected by EMU (see Hefeker 1996b). They might be wrong if the results of this chapter can be applied to other industries as well.

Notes

1. Of course, not all products of the banking industry are tradable. For the purpose of this study, however, I disregard the domestic part of the banking business.

2. In a neo-classical model this would raise the wage-rent ratio. Given the high unemployment in Europe, the benefits are likely to accrue to capital owners instead.

3. Canals (1993) describes in detail the declared strategies of the "Deutsche Bank" and the "Banque Nationale de Paris".

4. The complete list is Barclays, British Aerospace, British American Tobacco, British Petroleum, Citibank, Ernst and Young, Goldman Sachs, Imperial Chemical Industries, Midland Montagu, Salomon International, Shearson Brothers, and S. G. Warburg (Frieden 1991).

5. One might also expect that large banks have increasing returns to scale in transborder business as well. This would only strengthen the results derived here.

6. For a formal proof of the existence of such intervals, see Grüner and Hefeker (1996).

6

Bureaucratic Interests in Monetary Union: The Bundesbank

6.1. Introduction

The 1993 collapse of the European Monetary System (EMS) marks a setback in the movement towards European Monetary Union (EMU). The decision to adopt a 30 percent corridor around the bilateral target rate constitutes a step backwards on the way towards the full monetary union envisaged in the Maastricht Treaty. This development casts doubt about the future of the common monetary system and whether EMU will be reached according to the timetable determined in the Maastricht Treaty. After a successful history and following a time without realignments in the five years preceding September 1992, with the removal of capital controls and with new entrants into the Exchange Rate Mechanism (ERM), the question arises how this sudden shift can be explained.

The literature on this question identifies two major causes for the occurrence of the September 1992 crisis and the final collapse of the EMS on August 2, 1993.[1] One explanation identifies the large idiosyncratic shock of German unification as pivotal (Portes 1993). The "inconsistent trio" of stable exchange rates, independent monetary policy and free capital movements caused the collapse of the EMS, as the Bundesbank had to tighten monetary policy in reaction to excessive German government spending following unification, while the other EMS countries were unwilling to follow in tightening money supply, as well as to devalue. Another interpretation stresses the role of the Maastricht Treaty in this context. Eichengreen and Wyplosz (1993) view the treaty inducing rational balance of payments crises, causing the collapse. A speculative attack forcing a devaluation prevents a country from satisfying the non-devaluation requirement two years prior to EMU of the Maastricht Treaty. The country, once driven out of the EMS, no longer qualifies for EMU membership and has no incentive to continue a restrictive monetary policy. Moreover, as Alesina and Grilli (1993) argue, countries that are not in the first tier of EMU may be later politically rejected from those inside the union.[2] A speculative crisis could thus prove self-fulfilling.

Overall, the literature assigns only a passive role to the Bundesbank. I instead focus on the active role of the Bundesbank in the collapse of the EMS and suggest that the Bundesbank's self-interests might have been decisive for the collapse of the EMS. In this interpretation, the Bundesbank's behavior was caused by German Monetary Union (GMU) in combination with the Maastricht Treaty.

First, I argue that the chosen exchange rate between deutsche mark (DM) and ostmark in the course of German unification marked the starting point of a conflict between the German government and the Bundesbank. The Bundesbank had to accept a different rate of conversion than it had proposed and suffered a major loss in its reputation as an independent central bank *vis-à-vis* the German public and the EMS partners (see Marsh 1992). Expansionary fiscal policy adopted by the government only aggravated this conflict, being countered by tight monetary policy. Given the dominant role of the Bundesbank in the EMS and the constraints for independent monetary policy in the ERM, the tight German monetary policy spilled over into other ERM countries, forcing them to tighten monetary policy as well. While the European countries first profited from the export boom caused by German unification, with the upcoming recession the European governments were no longer able to defend the exchange rate by raising interest rates. The trade-off between the benefits of stable exchange rates and the costs of reduced monetary autonomy became steeper and it became more costly to trade the benefits of monetary union later for reduced autonomy and unemployment now.[3]

Following the real shock of the German unification, many observers were certain that the DM would revalue because of the capital inflows needed to rebuild East Germany (Melitz 1991; Wyplosz 1991). However France, as the major adversary of the Bundesbank, was unwilling to devalue its currency against the DM. Having adopted a policy of competitive disinflation in the second half of the 1980s (Blanchard and Muet 1993), France now wanted to receive the benefits of a low inflation rate, and also the prestige from having a more stable currency than Germany, hoping to become gradually the new "anchor" of the system. Hence, a devaluation against the DM was ruled out (Portes 1993). But when markets expected that politicians in ERM countries were no longer able to defend the exchange rate for domestic reasons, their one-way speculation resulted in too high a pressure to resist, magnified by the Bundesbank's reluctance to intervene and stabilize the exchange rate. Nearly one year earlier than France, Italy and Britain could no longer stand the incompatibility between domestic pressure and external prestige and devalued.

The second reason for the EMS collapse can be seen in the Maastricht Treaty itself. The treaty is often interpreted as stemming from German unification and signaling German commitment to the European unification process (Garrett 1993; Sandholtz 1993). By accepting a specific date for monetary union, Germany surrenders monetary autonomy as the price for the European countries', and especially the French, approval to German unification. I argue instead that the treaty, by fixing the date when the Bundesbank would lose independence and thus the leading role in Europe, prompted the Bundesbank to set monetary policy even tighter than it might have done otherwise. A relatively restrictive policy was regarded as a possibility to stop the movement towards EMU as growing domestic political pressures in the partner countries signaled that they would no longer be able to defend their exchange rate against the DM. The effects of GMU, in this perspective, only gave the Bundesbank a reason to block EMU after the Maastricht Treaty had been signed. Thus, the treaty, seen as a German commitment to European unification, actually triggered the EMS crisis and caused its collapse.

The chapter proceeds as follows. In Section 6.2, the GMU shock and the resulting conflict between the German government and the Bundesbank are described. In Sections 6.3 and 6.4, the external dimensions of GMU and the EMS crisis are addressed. Section 6.5 presents a model on the above considerations and the final section offers concluding comments.

6.2. The Role of German Monetary Union

After World War II and with a vivid memory of two major hyperinflations, there was a nearly unanimous consensus in Germany that stable and positive growth required a stable monetary policy. Even German trade unions never seriously doubted this basic concept of the "social market economy". Although there were minor conflicts between the both concerning the daily course of monetary policy (see Marsh 1992), the Bundesbank had always been careful not to push the conflict too hard out of the fear of losing its independence which is only granted by simple law (Goodman 1992; Hartwig 1984).[4] Although the Bundesbank is very self-confident concerning its independence, its behavioral independence changed over time. Already in 1956, the then German chancellor, Adenauer, had publicly questioned the independence of the then Bank deutscher Länder. His government also proposed a more centralized system for the Bundesbank, which was however rejected by the German federal states, the Länder (Lohmann 1993b).[5]

In its position *vis-à-vis* the government, nevertheless, the Bundesbank could always count on the public's support, which also restricted the government's possible actions. Vaubel (1993) argues that the Bundesbank mainly targeted public support and hence also bowed to political pressure when it feared to lose public support for its policy. Empirical evidence for this argument can be found in Frey and Schneider (1981). Goodman (1992) argues along the same lines and cites events when the Bundesbank eased monetary policy as well as times when the Bundesbank preferred to demonstrate its independence and undermined the government's policy (see also Hartwig 1984, and Marsh 1992). The Bundesbank as a bureaucratic institution hence followed its own aims, demonstrating its independence when possible but taking into account the government's threat to take away independence when conflicts became too severe.

This rather non-conflictual relationship changed drastically with the occurrence of German Monetary Union, after which the German government offended the Bundesbank with its choice of the rate of conversion between ostmark and deutsche mark and by embarking on a course of excessive fiscal spending.

The Government's Political Interests

Preceding monetary union, already with the fall of the Berlin Wall a lively discussion started among economists about the right form of economic integration between the two Germanys. Much of the academic discussion was concentrated on the appropriate rate of conversion of ostmark stocks and flows into DM after West Germany's chancellor Kohl in February 1990 had proposed monetary union for July 1990. This discussion was influenced considerably by the experience with the West German currency reform of 1948 and the fear of an inflationary impact of too generous a conversion rate. As several authors point out (e.g. Neumann 1992), the absence of a free market economy and price-setting implied that there was no sound basis to determine the equilibrium rate of conversion. The choice then was necessarily an arbitrary one. For reasons of East Germany's competitiveness, economists proposed an exchange rate between DM and ostmark in the range of 1:2 and 1:5, while the optimal choice was seen in a slight undervaluation (see e.g. Siebert 1991). The Bundesbank instead was more concerned with the conversion of money stocks and voiced its fear of the inflationary consequences of a 1:1 conversion of savings and debts, because socialist countries were usually characterized by a huge monetary overhang which could result in a surge of inflation. Thus, the Bundesbank proposed a rate of conversion of 2:1, which it regarded already as a compromise, preferring an even higher rate of conversion (Marsh 1992, Chapter 8).

The final decision of the German government, however, which is the exchange rate authority in Germany, resulted in a weighted average between 1.8:1 and 1.6:1.[6] It was a political choice, obviously caused by election motives (von Hagen 1992) and an attempt to restrict migration from the East to the West. The first general elections for the united Germany were set for December 1990 and it thus seemed safer to show generous behavior *vis-à-vis* the new citizens by converting the majority of private stocks 1:1. This decision resulted in an increase in money supply (M3) of approximately DM 180 billion. This level effect, however, did not bring about the feared inflationary impulse. Thus, the financial markets' skepticism, which was reflected in an immediate jump of the long-term interest rate by 150 basis points after the announcement of monetary union, turned out to be exaggerated. Higher inflation did not show up immediately after unification because excess supply in EMS partner countries helped to supply the Eastern market and to satisfy the excess demand for consumer durables (Kröger and Teutemann 1992).

Not only was the rate of conversion caused by reelection motives of the German government, but, and more drastically, the change in the fiscal policy afterwards. The asymmetric conversion of ostmark liabilities and assets directly caused additional public deficits of about DM 30 billion because the federal budgets had to cover the gap. Moreover, the generous conversion of not only stocks but also flows (wages, pensions etc.) led to high expenditures on East German transfer payments and salaries. Rapidly increasing wages also caused unemployment, in addition to a loss of exports to former trading partners in the socialist-bloc, raising transfer payments even more. Moreover, several investment subsidies and tax exemptions to foster investment in East Germany were designed (Kröger and Teutemann 1992: 36).

Fiscal policy thus reflected the classical motive of creating a political business cycle (see Chapter 2). While the rapidly rising wages in East Germany caused a major wave of unemployment, the government had to ensure winning the next elections. For this reason, a tremendous program of public spending was launched. Public construction, subsidies, employment programs etc. were not only created for the eastern part of the country but also continued without restriction in West Germany. Government transfers from West Germany were also needed for financing most of the expenditures of the new state and local governments in the East (Siebert 1991). Consequently, the budget deficit soared, as increased spending was mainly financed by public debt instead of tax revenue. Deficit spending resulted in increased pressure on the price level that was aggravated by the post-unification boom in West Germany over the following years and the continuously rising wages in both parts of the country beyond increases in productivity (Franz et al. 1993). This posed considerable problems for monetary stability in Germany. Consequently, the Bundesbank warned repeatedly that the loosening of fiscal policy might create a severe danger for the stability of the DM (see e.g. the Bundesbank's Monthly Report of October 1991). The Bundesbank's reaction to this policy shift will now be examined.

The Bundesbank's Reaction

Monetary union confronted the Bundesbank with severe problems. Although a conversion of stocks does not *per se* increase the rate of inflation (Sargent and Velde 1990), the problems of the Bundesbank were more difficult. In addition to a signal extraction problem, because private agents might not be able to distinguish between a one-time price level adjustment and a rise in the rate of inflation, resulting in a rise of expected inflation, the Bundesbank also faced the problem of an unknown money demand function in the new territories. The unexpectedly large increase in the money supply could either be a larger-than-expected demand for money or reflect the buildup of an inflationary potential.[7] Both effects gave the Bundesbank an incentive to suppress even these adjustment effects, as if it were a rise in the rate of inflation, to secure the long-run credibility of its price-stability commitment. Its desire to keep its prestige as an inflation fighter might have resulted in a "contractive bias" (von Hagen 1992: 214). The biggest problem, nevertheless, was posed by the development of the public finances after unification.

Thus, partly justified by real problems of information uncertainty, partly caused by the determination to defend its reputation, the Bundesbank reacted extremely cautionary. Another reason for tightening money supply was probably due to the fact that the Bundesbank felt humiliated by the government. While officially the question of the correct exchange rate was still under discussion, the chancellor announced his decision on the exchange rate, without informing the Bundesbank's president Karl-Otto Pöhl (Marsh 1992).[8] This public neglect of the Bundesbank's intentions and concerns might have caused the Bundesbank to demonstrate its determination to defend the value of the DM nevertheless and to compensate for lost prestige in Germany.

Moreover, the German government embarked on the Maastricht process that is usually seen as a German commitment to European unification (Sandholtz 1992; Garrett 1993). The Bundesbank, however, interpreted this as an attempt to trade its autonomy for political aims. As the treaty foresaw monetary union to begin by 1999 at the latest, at the same time the Bundesbank saw its stabilization successes and its independence threatened. The Maastricht Treaty of December 1991 provided the Bundesbank hence with yet one more reason to tighten monetary policy. Being the leader of the EMS central banks and also the "guardian" of an important international currency, the Bundesbank directors had to defend their international reputation and the "anchor" role of the DM. The Bundesbank had adopted the idea and position of being the monetary anchor of Europe and often referred to this role, stressing the importance of keeping this position especially after GMU. Nevertheless, after the Delors Report, the Bundesbank had also consistently expressed its reservation *vis-à-vis* the idea of EMU. It claimed to need independence to continue its stable monetary policy and voiced its fear of being constrained in this aim by less stability-oriented countries in a common monetary authority.

After the Delors Report had been published, criticism and objections increased and were repeated continuously. Still, however, the Bundesbank could obviously live with the idea of monetary union in some distant future which was regarded as a rather theoretical construction without any practical meaning. With the Maastricht Treaty this position changed overnight. Now the Bundesbank could see that it would lose independence by January 1999 at the latest.[9] With the fixed date visible, the Bundesbank embarked on a course of defending its independence by obstructing this process. A new chance was seen to secure independence beyond 1997 or 1999. Hence, not only could monetary tightness rebuild lost reputation and heal the public humiliation, but it also constituted a possibility to hinder the Maastricht process using the inflationary effects of fiscal expansion as a reason for this policy.

Only one week after the Maastricht meeting the Bundesbank started to raise its interest rates trying thereby to make it more difficult for other countries to follow and fulfill the criteria of the treaty, thereby delaying the monetary union (Vaubel 1994). As a major recession was already visible on the European horizon, it was only a matter of time when the EMS partner countries would have to surrender their interest rate policy for domestic reasons. Given a major recession, almost no country is able to keep interest rates high only to defend an, obviously biased, exchange rate. Lost jobs and election motives will eventually prove to be more important. I now turn to the policy reactions of the EMS countries.

6.3. External Effects of GMU

For the Bundesbank and the EMS partners, upon unification the question arose whether macroeconomic shocks following German unification required an exchange rate adjustment. The need for a real appreciation would sooner or later also imply a nominal appreciation.[10] Thus, the Bundesbank proposed a general realignment of the EMS which, in its perspective, would also have helped to reduce the pressure on the price level in Germany as a larger part of the demand shock would be shifted onto the European partners. The EMS countries in contrast were not interested in a realignment. Although they lamented the policy mix adopted in Germany, they saw no possibility to loosen the close interest rate connection (Bofinger 1991a). At least for the so-called weak currency countries this would have resulted in an increased risk premium on interest rates. As already explained, especially France opposed the idea of devaluation as the policy of the *franc forte* had become the centerpiece of French economic policy. France hoped to become the new "anchor" of the system (see The Economist, June 26, 1993: 90). The Bundesbank, in turn, did not want to allow real appreciation to come about by German inflation (Portes 1993). This implied deflation for the other countries as Germany's price level had to rise relatively to the rest of the EMS.

While the spill-over effects of the interest rate increase hit the partner countries hard, forcing them to raise interest rates to defend their currencies *vis-à-vis* the DM, Germany also worked as a locomotive for their exports. The demand pull effect of unification, in a situation of nearly full capacity-utilization in West Germany, met favorably with declining capacity utilization in Europe and the U.S. The EC countries started to export their excess production to Germany. Accordingly, the German current account surplus from 1989 turned into a deficit in 1991. Several countries even spurred their exports to Germany on a two-digit basis.[11] Eichengreen and Wyplosz (1993), however, also report some competitiveness problems for Italy, Spain and Great Britain which might be due to insufficient price decreases.

In conclusion, a nominal appreciation of the DM had made it much easier for the other EMS countries to achieve real depreciation as it had reduced the necessary amount of deflation. That this did not happen is caused by the reputational conflict between France and the Bundesbank about the anchor currency of the EMS. Thus, the cooperative feature of the EMS was destroyed, leading markets to anticipate a future policy shift as domestic conditions in EMS countries worsened, implying the loss of credibility for the EMS. The breakdown of the EMS was expedited by the Bundesbank's unwillingness (Vaubel 1994), or inability (Portes 1993) to intervene in defense of other currencies.

6.4. The Story of Two Crises

The rejection of the Maastricht Treaty in the Danish referendum in June 1992 marked the starting point of the first crisis, triggering expectations among speculators that the monetary union would be delayed beyond the date set by the Maastricht Treaty (Eichengreen and Wyplosz 1993).[12] Speculations against the weaker currencies of the EMS followed immediately. Despite intervention the Italian lira fell towards its lower limit. The currencies in the wider band (pound, peseta, escudo) fell as well. The pressure increased with the French referendum approaching in August and September. The crisis then actually worsened from outside the EMS. On September 8, the Finnish marka suspended its unilateral peg to the ECU. Already in November 1991 it had been forced to devalue by 12 percent, due to the collapse of Soviet trade and a domestic banking crisis. Following the marka, the Swedish krona came under attack. The Reiksbank was forced to raise the interest rate to three-digit levels (the overnight rate rose to 500 percent). As it was only a unilateral peg without financing facilities and intervention, pressures could not be tamed.

Thereafter, speculation turned to the EMS as doubts about exchange rate bands in general arose. Despite Italian interest rate increases and intervention by partner countries, the lira devalued on September 13. This first realignment in five years only triggered further speculation against the weaker currencies and new entrants. Pressure on the pound, peseta and escudo mounted, while that on the lira continued. Three days later, the ERM membership of the British pound was suspended and two interest rate increases in Britain were reversed. Italy followed the British example and the Spanish peseta devalued 5 percent. The narrow positive outcome of the French referendum of September 20 only intensified speculation. France was forced to increase its interest rates and to intervene heavily. Pressure spread to the Belgian franc; Spain, Portugal and Ireland reintroduced or sharpened capital controls. In November, Sweden abandoned the unilateral peg followed by new pressure on the Danish krone and the Iberian currencies. The krone could be defended but the escudo and the peseta both experienced a 6 percent devaluation. In December, Norway surrendered its peg, causing renewed pressures on the French franc and the Irish punt. The franc was defended but the punt was devalued in January 1994.

Eichengreen and Wyplosz (1993) provide an interesting overview about the judgement of market participants concerning the exchange crisis of 1992. They asked market dealers about the reasons for the crisis. Those identified the lack of public support for the Maastricht Treaty and high German interest rates as the main reasons for speculation against the weaker currencies. Those high interest rates were no longer deemed to be politically feasible. They also point out that central banks' reserves are more vulnerable since capital controls are largely absent in Europe.

The second crisis, once again, started at the fringes of the ERM. The release of rising unemployment figures in Spain in February triggered sellings of the peseta. In May, it had to be devalued another 8 percent. Portugal, although not under such pressures, followed suit and devalued 6.5 percent. Both countries then used the gained room to lower interest rates. In central Europe the recession, spreading from the U.S. and the UK, gathered force. Although France expressed determination to defend the franc, gloomy reports on the French economy triggered pressure on the franc in July. The Bundesbank intervened heavily, resulting in tremendous increases in foreign currency reserves. As markets realized that again in July the German money supply rose by more than expected, it became clear that the Bundesbank would not be willing to lower interest rates. Although observers were convinced that a full percent lowering of the German interest rates was necessary to release pressure on the franc, making it politically possible for France to remain in the ERM, the Bundesbank declined to do so (Eichengreen 1993c; Svensson 1994).[13] Massive intervention ensued, and by the end of July the Bank of France had run down its reserves, while those of the Bundesbank rose by nearly DM 40 billion. This increase, if not sterilized, posed a danger to the money supply in Germany, and the Bundesbank was thus unwilling to intervene any further (Vaubel 1994).

However, only unsterilized intervention might have kept the markets from continued speculation. But from the launching of the EMS in 1979 onwards, the Bundesbank had never accepted the obligation of unsterilized and unrestricted intervention (see Eichengreen and Wyplosz 1993). Kenen (1995a, b) points out the importance of the so-called Emminger letter. This letter conceded to the Bundesbank that when intervention requirements and internal price stability conflicted, the latter would take precedence. It had been demanded by the then Bundesbank president Otmar Emminger who signed the EMS act. Kenen argues that this letter was invoked by the Bundesbank in the 1993 crisis, granting the possibility to decline further intervention. That the intervention of the Bundesbank was not unrestricted might well have influenced the expectations of markets when the conflict between the Bundesbank's objectives and the needs of the EMS became evident.

The last weekend in July then saw the historical meeting of European finance ministers and central bankers. The central bankers proposed two ways out of the crisis. They proposed either to generally widen the band to around 6 percent or to allow the DM to leave the ERM. While France was skeptical that 6 percent would be enough, the Benelux countries refused to let the DM float against their currencies. The final decision brought the widening of the bands to ±15 percent.

Several explanations for the occurrence of both crises have been suggested. While some focus on the underlying real problems stemming from GMU (Portes 1992; Vaubel 1994), others (Gros 1992; Eichengreen and Wyplosz 1993) apply the literature of balance of payments crises (see Krugman 1979; Obstfeld 1986) to explain the dissolution of the tight exchange rate band. These explanations, of course, are not mutually exclusive. Speculation might explain the timing of both crises, as growing unemployment and the recession would not explain the specific date for the outbreak of speculation. The referenda in Denmark and France, nevertheless, signaled growing public objection to the Maastricht Treaty and its constraints for monetary policy, indicating that governments might soon be forced to give up their EMS membership. Moreover, tight monetary policy set in EMS countries to defend their currencies might have actually accelerated the crisis. As Drazen and Masson (1994) explain, a deflationary policy might lead markets to expect an earlier reversal of policy as political pressures increase.

There are also several interpretations why the crises occurred in two stages. Eichengreen and Wyplosz (1993) suggest that France and the Benelux countries were nearer to the center of the EMS and thus to the Bundesbank's policy. Another, not incompatible interpretation, might be that Italy and Britain were the EMS's weakest members and thus easier to push out for the Bundesbank. Moreover, the role of different EMS preferences might help to explain this two-stage dissolution.

The developments after the collapse have been frequently interpreted as proof that the speculation, at least against the franc, had not been justified. The Banque de France did not lower its interest rates and remained more or less in the tight corridor to the DM. Moreover, wider margins reduced the risk premia on other currencies which in turn might have enabled these partners to withstand domestic political pressure. It is possible that especially France could handle a level of interest rates comparable to the German level, but not one, caused by market expectations, which is considerably higher (Eichengreen 1993c). Another interpretation for the stable relations after the collapse might be the Bundesbank's reaction. After having forced the EMS currencies out and having shattered the ERM, it soon had space, and used it, to relax German monetary policy and to reduce the interest rate gaps. Already on August 3, it cut its repurchase rate, followed by another cut one day later, citing as a reason its aim to calm the foreign exchange markets. It also announced that it would use all scope to further cut interest rates (The Economist, August 7, 1993: 22). One might also conclude, however, that after having shattered the ERM, there was no longer the necessity to be too restrictive in setting monetary policy.

6.5. Modeling the EMS Collapse

In this section, a simple model is presented to analyze the policies of the relevant actors leading to the collapse of the EMS. I use a game-theoretical model with imperfect information that is solved by backward induction to describe the behavior of the actors. It is similar to the model developed in Chapter 2 but simplified to an aggregate output aim. Again, a political aim is added to the economic aims of the actors.

The German government, as represented by the fiscal authority, is concerned with inflation and output. Given its politically determined short-time horizon as elections approach, it is predominantly concerned with output because higher output enhances the chances of reelection. Increasing government expenditures would expand output, while the inflationary effect is only felt after a certain time-lag. The central bank in contrast has a longer time-horizon. Given its function as "protector of the currency" it is primarily concerned with monetary stability, placing less weight on the output target than the government. The employees of the central bank derive their prestige and utility from keeping the price level stable. Price stability, which gives the assurance of having performed well, is their most important goal (Andersen and Schneider 1986).

The German government's objective function is given by

(6.1) $$V = -\left[\alpha\left(y - \overline{y}\right)^2 + \beta\pi^2\right] + \lambda D \,,$$

with

(6.2) $$y = a_1 g + a_2 m - \varepsilon \,,$$

and

(6.3) $$\pi = b_1 g + b_2 m \,,$$

where utility, again expressed as political support, is a negative function of deviations from the full employment target level $\overline{y}$ and of inflation π (the preferred rate of which is zero).[14] To this standard formulation of the government's objective function I add λD, which is a weighted dummy for EMS membership, signifying the desire to achieve European integration and to signal Germany's commitment to it. D takes the value of one with the signing of the Maastricht Treaty and is zero before. In this short-term model, increases in output and employment y in the united Germany are a positive function of government spending g and an increase in the money supply m. Output is negatively affected by the external shock of German unification ε.[15] Equation (6.3) shows that government spending and monetary expansion both increase inflation. All parameters are positive. It is assumed that government spending has a stronger impact on employment than on inflation, while the opposite is true for money supply.

The Bundesbank's objective function is given by

(6.4) $$U = -\left[\gamma\left(y - \overline{y}\right)^2 + \delta\pi^2\right] - \mu D \,.$$

In comparison with the government, the Bundesbank is assumed to place relatively more value on the inflation aim and relatively less value on the employment aim. The second source of conflict is constituted by the negative value of the Maastricht Treaty here because the Bundesbank's utility is not only dependent on stable prices but also on independence. Monetary union would instead endanger the possibility to set the most preferred rate of money supply and thus undermine the prestige derived from low inflation. Even a low European rate of inflation would no longer be attributed to the Bundesbank, while in the pre-Maastricht EMS the Bundesbank was viewed as exerting a disciplinary pressure on other countries. All these effects are captured by the dummy D, which is one for the envisaged loss of independence by monetary union and zero before the Maastricht Treaty.

The Policy Consensus Before GMU

Before the shock of German economic and monetary union, the German government and the Bundesbank cooperatively set their respective policies. In contrast to similar models where authorities act cooperatively because of the Pareto-efficiency (Andersen and Schneider 1986), the reason here for both to play cooperatively is found in their. Each player chooses a cooperative solution because the game is repeated. Although the German government has an incentive to renege on the agreement given its short time-horizon, it is also aware that the Bundesbank receives a high rate of approval by the German public. Given this stability consensus, the government does not risk a confrontation with the Bundesbank in normal times, that is without the shock ε. The Bundesbank in turn has no incentive to renege on the agreement because it cannot risk too strong a conflict with the government, fearing the loss of independence which is granted only by simple law (Goodman 1992). Moreover, given the government's consideration of the stability consensus, the Bundesbank can perform well enough in a cooperative game without confronting the government and the risk of losing independence. The model here abstracts from the occasional conflicts before GMU described in Section 6.2.

Before the external shock of German unification (ε=0) and the Maastricht Treaty (D=0), it is thus assumed that the German government and the Bundesbank cooperate and maximize a common objective function because the major sources of conflict are absent. Their common objective function is a weighted average of both individual objective functions:

$$(6.5) \qquad VU = \Theta V + (1 - \Theta)U .$$

The actual outcome of the joint maximization is determined by joint maximization of the authorities. Using equations (6.2) and (6.3) in (6.1) and (6.4) and combining them in (6.5) gives the optimal cooperative choice of the instruments as

$$(6.6) \qquad g_c = \overset{-}{y} \left[\frac{b_2 (b_2 a_1 - b_1 a_2)}{(b_2 a_1)^2 + (b_1 a_2)^2 - \tau} \right] ,$$

and

(6.7)
$$m_c = y \left[\frac{b_1(b_1 a_2 - b_2 a_1)}{(b_2 a_1)^2 + (b_1 a_2)^2 - \tau} \right],$$

with $\tau = 2a_1 a_2 b_1 b_2$, where the index c refers to the cooperative setting of the instrument.

The Foreign Authority and the Recession

The foreign EMS country, denoted by asterisks, is assumed to profit from the Maastricht Treaty. The treaty provides a possibility to increase the credibility of stability-oriented monetary policy, while on the other hand to gain influence on the setting of European monetary policy. This, for reasons of reputation, might be especially important for France (De Grauwe 1993). The foreign EMS country's objective function is therefore given by

(6.8)
$$V^* = -\left[\alpha^* \left(y^* - \overline{y^*} \right)^2 + \beta^* \pi^{*2} \right] + \lambda^* D,$$

where the dummy captures the value of being in the EMS. The relative weight λ^* placed on the dummy is allowed to vary between countries to reflect diverging preferences of different EMS countries regarding EMS membership. The monetary and fiscal instruments, for simplicity, are assumed to have the same relative impact on employment and inflation as in the German case. It is assumed that in the foreign country only one authority, the fiscal authority as a government agency, decides over both instruments so that no conflict between central bank and fiscal authority arises. This assumption reflects the institutional facts in most of the EMS countries in 1992/93, when most of the central banks had not yet received political independence, although the Maastricht Treaty requires independence for all central banks before entry into EMU.

In the case of the European recession, the negative external shock ξ, the foreign government may choose to leave the EMS, in which case

(6.9)
$$y^* = a_1 g^* + a_2 m^* - \xi,$$

and

(6.10)
$$\pi^* = b_1 g^* + b_2 m^*$$

are domestically determined.[16] This allows the stabilization of output and employment by increasing the money supply, hence maximizing government utility according to preferences. The costs, however, are increased inflation and an EMS dummy of zero value.

The EMS membership valued positively, to qualify for EMU and secure an influence on European monetary policy later, there is an incentive to stay in the EMS. Then, however, monetary policy cannot be independently set. The foreign money supply is tied by $m^* = \varphi m$ to the German money supply, where φ describes the tightness of the exchange rate constraint. If φ is equal to one, the foreign money supply is tied completely to the German one, leaving no discretion. With $\varphi > 1$ some discretion is given for the foreign authority. Consequently

$$(6.9') \qquad y^* = a_1 g^* + a_2 \varphi m - \xi$$

and

$$(6.10') \qquad \pi^* = b_1 g^* + b_2 \varphi m$$

illustrate the EMS case.

To keep the analysis simple, it is assumed that when the negative external shock for the foreign country ξ is zero, the EMS solution will always be chosen because reneging bears credibility costs for the government. This implies that the relative weight λ^* of the EMS dummy is high enough to compensate for lost autonomy. When the shock occurs, however, the foreign authority has to decide whether to choose m^* independently and to stabilize output by increasing the money supply or to stay in the EMS and adopt the Bundesbank's monetary policy φm. For the simplicity of the analysis, I set g^* constant for both cases so that the foreign authority's decision depends solely on the money supply. This may reflect a certain institutional constraint which, for example, requires the level of government spending not to surpass a certain value, the slow working of the budgetary process, or an external borrowing constraint.

The foreign authority's decision will of course depend on which choice yields higher utility. The decision problem is consequently

$$(6.11) \quad \max_{m} \; V_m^*(\xi) = \begin{cases} -\left[\alpha^*\left(y^* - \overline{y\,*}\right)^2 + \beta^*\pi^{*2}\right], & \text{for } m^* > \varphi m \\[2mm] -\left[\alpha^*\left(y^* - \overline{y\,*}\right)^2 + \beta^*\pi^{*2}\right] + \lambda^* D, & \text{for } m^* = \varphi m \end{cases}$$

The difference in both utilities for setting money supply under the EMS constraint or independently is now evaluated for the case of the shock. First, the optimal value of money supply for the unconstrained case is calculated by using equations (6.8), (6.9), (6.10) and differentiating $U^*(\xi)$ with respect to m^*. This yields an optimal increase in money supply of

$$(6.12) \qquad \tilde{m}^*(\xi) = \frac{\alpha^* a_2\left(\xi + \overline{y\,*}\right) - g^*\left(\alpha^* a_2 a_1 + \beta^* b_2 b_1\right)}{\upsilon^*},$$

where $\upsilon^* = \alpha^* a_2^2 + \beta^* b_2^2$. The tilde characterizes the optimal unconstrained value of the instrument in case of a shock. Whether utility is higher when staying in the EMS or when leaving it is, of course, dependent on the German money supply that determines the difference between $\tilde{m}^*$ and φm. Comparing utility levels for $\tilde{m}^*$ and φm by using equation (11) results in the following. The foreign authority will opt for $\tilde{m}^*$ and leave the EMS if $V^*(\tilde{m}) - V^*(\varphi m) - \lambda^* D \geq 0$.[17] This is the case if

$$(6.13) \qquad \varphi m \geq \tilde{m}^* + \left(\frac{\lambda^*}{\upsilon^*}\right)^{\!\!\frac{1}{2}}.$$

Note that both the value placed on the EMS membership λ^* and the monetary policy constraint φ play an important role in the decision of the foreign government. Different values of λ^* for individual countries capture different attitudes towards EMS membership and the importance placed upon it. Only when the difference between the adequate money supply to counter the negative shock and the money supply tied to the Bundesbank is sufficiently large will the foreign country opt out.

The Bundesbank's Choice

When the German government confronts the Bundesbank with uncooperative behavior, the Bundesbank in turn no longer sets its money supply cooperatively. It now has the chance to optimize its utility function without restriction, because the Maastricht Treaty, while implying the loss of independence by 1999, requires also all countries to grant independence to their central banks before entering EMU. This requirement widens the range of possible actions for the Bundesbank as it takes away the threat of losing independence when confronting the government. Moreover, the problems of monetary control stemming from German Monetary Union (see von Hagen 1992) give an excuse to be too restrictive. Finally, the Bundesbank can count on increasing public opposition to the Maastricht Treaty because of increasing rates of unemployment (Marsh 1992).

By using equations (6.2), (6.3) and (6.4), the unconstrained optimization of its objective function yields

(6.14)
$$\tilde{m} = \frac{\gamma a_2 \left(\varepsilon + \bar{y} \right) - g \left(\gamma a_2 a_1 + \delta b_2 b_1 \right)}{\omega},$$

with $\omega = \gamma a_2^2 + \delta b_2^2$.

The non-cooperative solution, however, provides the Bundesbank with yet another possibility, as it is now totally unrestricted in choosing $\tilde{m}$. Knowing that under certain circumstances the foreign government will rather leave the EMS to stabilize output, the Bundesbank sees an opportunity to push the foreign country out and thereby reduce the probability of monetary union or at least hinder the process towards it. This can be achieved by tightening $\tilde{m}$ even a bit further.[18] Assuming that the Bundesbank knows the critical difference between $\tilde{m}^*$ and φm for the foreign country, given the shock ξ, it can calculate a money supply tight enough to establish its aim of EMS collapse.

The critical value of its own money supply for which the foreign authority will drop out of the EMS is, by inverting (6.13), defined to be

(6.15)
$$\bar{m} \equiv \frac{\tilde{m}^*(\xi) + \left(\lambda^* / \upsilon^* \right)^{1/2}}{\varphi}.$$

That is, for any $m < \bar{m}$ set by the Bundesbank, the foreign authority will exit from the EMS.

When setting its monetary target after GMU, however, the Bundesbank is uncertain whether the shock ξ will occur. Nevertheless, it has to choose the course of its future monetary policy and to stick to it in order to defend its already damaged reputation. Yet the Bundesbank knows that with a certain probability P an adverse shock ξ will occur in the form of a recession that spills over to Europe. (The other countries know of course about the occurrence of the shock when making their decision.) P can either be seen as the probability of the occurrence of a shock or, alternatively, as uncertainty concerning the magnitude of the shock that gives the opportunity to drive the foreign country out of the EMS. Thus the Bundesbank's expected utility is given by

$$(6.16) \qquad \underset{m}{EU} = PU(m) + (1 - P)[U(m) - \mu D],$$

with $m = \begin{cases} \leq \overline{m} \\ \underline{}, \\ > \overline{m} \end{cases}$ where P is the exogenous probability that $\xi = 1$ and (1-P) is

the probability that $\xi = 0$. (6.16) captures the possibility of driving other countries out, given the occurrence of the shock, but also depicts the risk of setting money too tight when no shock occurs. By comparing its utility levels $[U(\tilde{m}) - EU(\overline{m})]$, the Bundesbank will set $\overline{m}$ if

$$(6.17) \qquad \overline{m} \geq \tilde{m} + \left(\frac{P\mu}{\omega}\right)^{\!\frac{1}{2}}.$$

According to equation (6.17), important factors for the Bundesbank are the probability P that ξ occurs and the (negative) value the Bundesbank places on the EMS goal. If the unconstrained money supply $\tilde{m}$ is sufficiently large, the Bundesbank will prefer not to lose public support in Germany by being restrictive and let thus the other country stay in the EMS. If, however, $\tilde{m}$ is small, the Bundesbank will set $\overline{m}$. In this case the EMS will dissolve.

The Government's Choice

The German government, faced with the adverse shock of German unification ε and knowing the reaction of the Bundesbank, has to decide whether to break the agreement with the Bundesbank, even if this will imply a relatively tighter money supply, making even more fiscal spending necessary as it undermines the positive effects of $\tilde{g}$. Moreover, it knows that this might also endanger the future of the EMS. In the case of a negative shock for the foreign authority, the Bundesbank might take the chance to dissolve the EMS by making its monetary policy excessively restrictive. Thus, the government must not only decide about the future relationship with its own central bank when breaking the implicit contract with it, but also on the external effects of its policy choice.

The government's decision problem is thus given by

$$(6.18) \qquad \max \; V(\varepsilon) = \begin{cases} \underset{g_\varepsilon}{V}(g_\varepsilon, m_\varepsilon), & \text{for } m = m_\varepsilon \\[2mm] \underset{\widetilde{g}}{E}V(\widetilde{g}, m), & \text{with } m = \begin{cases} \widehat{m} \\[1mm] \overline{m} \end{cases} \end{cases}$$

The government has to compare the utility derived from continuing the co-operative policy with regard to the Bundesbank, in which case g_c is relevant, or to set $\widetilde{g}$ in a non-cooperative manner. In the second case, expected utility is dependent on the choice of the Bundesbank's money supply. By using (6.1), (6.2) and (6.3), the non-cooperative choice of government spending is given as

$$(6.19) \qquad \widetilde{g} = \frac{\alpha a_1 (\varepsilon + \overline{y}) - m(\alpha a_1 a_2 + \beta b_1 b_2)}{\rho}$$

with $\rho = \alpha a_1^2 + \beta b_1^2$.

By comparing utility levels $[\, V(g_c) + \lambda D - V(\widetilde{g}) \,]^{19}$, the government will decide to play non-cooperatively if

$$(6.20) \qquad \widetilde{g} \geq g_c + (m_c - m)\left(\frac{\upsilon}{\rho}\right)^{\!\!\frac{1}{2}} + \left(\frac{\lambda}{\rho}\right)^{\!\!\frac{1}{2}}.$$

with $\upsilon = \alpha a_2^2 + \beta b_2^2$. In this case, the reelection motive of the German government is strong enough for it to break cooperation with the Bundesbank, although it knows that this may instigate the possible collapse of the EMS. According to this perspective, the German government embarked on the Maastricht accord to signal its commitment to European unity all the while knowing that its own action in the course of German unification could incur the risk of breaking the treaty. One could thus also place the blame for the EMS collapse mainly on the German government, whose actions prompted the Bundesbank to use its independence to obstruct the Maastricht process. One might speculate that, had the government not signed the treaty as a compensation to other European countries for their acceptance of German unification and had it not confronted the Bundesbank when deciding on the conversion rate, the EMS might still be intact. That the German government actually sought the EMS collapse to undermine the whole process of European integration, however, seems too strong a conclusion, as German industry, being an important interest group, is dependent on European trade relations, as Chapter 4 argued.

6.6. Conclusion

The model in this chapter focused on the interests of bureaucrats with regard to EMU, but it presents only one possible way to understand the events in Europe after German unification, which eventually led to the EMS crises and collapse. It does not necessarily contradict other interpretations. If speculative attacks brought down the EMS, then the Bundesbank influenced the expectations of the markets accordingly by signaling that it would not lend unrestricted support to the EMS and that it would not support the policies of the other countries by lowering its own interest rate either. Whether the markets forced the collapse of the EMS or politicians in other countries deliberately decided to leave the EMS is not crucial to my argument. I only argue that the Bundesbank created the environment for either action.

The model, although speculative, is consistent with the facts and events leading to the EMS-collapse. The behavior and statements by the Bundesbank are supportive of this interpretation. Especially the fact that it lowered its interest rates right after having achieved its aim supports the hypothesis advanced here.

This analysis sheds light on the decisive role one crucial actor, the Bundesbank, might have played in the EMS collapse and is thereby a first step towards closing an important gap in the literature. The important lesson from the recent crises is that more attention must be directed towards diverging interests of independent authorities like central banks. Although no one may doubt the benefits of an independent central bank, one should also be attentive to the fact that the bureaucracy central bank can obstruct politically set decisions out of pure self-interest and thus undermine international agreements. Ironically, the Maastricht Treaty which requires independent central banks for monetary stability may eventually result in more such problems when central banks try to realize their own objectives. (See Kenen 1992, on the democratic deficit of the planned European Central Bank.)

Notes

1. Throughout this chapter I interpret the widening of the bands of the ERM as the collapse of the EMS although it is not officially resolved. The ERM is, among the ECU

and credit provisions, only part of the EMS. Moreover, the Greek drachma was not included in the ERM. See Fratianni and von Hagen (1992), Giavazzi and Giovannini (1989), Gros and Thygesen (1992) for details.

2. As Kenen (1995b) points out, the Maastricht Treaty does not give the inside countries legal power to do this, because membership in EMU is automatic once the entry criteria are fulfilled.

3. Ozkan and Sutherland (1995) show how the time-horizon of politicians influences the stability of fixed exchange rates. With elections being near or in a strong recession the time-horizon might be considerably shortened.

4. The launching of the EMS in 1979 is sometimes also interpreted as an attempt by the German government to restrict the Bundesbank's power via the ERM (Vaubel 1980).

5. However, the German constitutional court ruled in 1962 that a change of the Bundesbank law would not have to be approved by the German federal states. Hence the central government could change that law on its own (Lohmann 1993b).

6. Most of the literature refers to a rate of 1.8:1. This, however, overlooks a special item in the balance of the East German banking system before conversion which was not converted. See Bofinger (1991a) for details.

7. The initial money endowment with 14.7 percent of West Germany's M3 was more than expected because the East German Staatsbank had misled the Bundesbank by treating foreign trade companies as banks. Likewise, the East German GDP was only 9.5 percent of West Germany's in contrast to the believed 14.5 percent based on wrong national accounting data (see Neumann 1992).

8. Marsh (1992, Chapter 8) describes in detail how the Bundesbank members expressed their feeling of humiliation and voiced publicly their critique about the government's disregard of the Bundesbank's autonomy. This treatment of the Bundesbank prompted Pöhl to resign few weeks later.

9. Several times the Bundesbank members stressed that there should not be a fixed timetable for monetary union but rather should it be dependent on economic criteria and convergence among member states (see e.g. Bundesbank, Auszüge aus Presseartikeln, Sept. 6, 1990).

10. On the other hand one might expect that demand for foreign goods as import restrictions for east Germans fall, will lead to a current account deficit that lowers the external value of the DM. In the long run the DM will have to depreciate because the external debt necessary for financing the integration of East Germany will have to be paid off. The then necessary current account surplus will require a depreciated DM as Melitz (1991) and Wyplosz (1991) argue.

11. It is a disputed issue whether the overall effect from GMU for the partner countries was a positive or a negative one. While some studies suggest that the adverse interest rate effects were larger (Hughes Hallett and Ma 1993), others conclude that the export boom had a larger positive effect (Franz et al. 1993).

12. Both crises are described in detail by Eichengreen (1993c), Kenen (1995b) and Svensson (1994).

13. Although the repurchasing and the lombard rate were cut, this was regarded as inadequate.

14. Note that the assumed preferred rate of zero inflation for the government excludes the motive to reduce real government debt via inflation as well as the seigniorage motive. The same assumption is made for the foreign government. Hence, I assume a European stability consensus where zero inflation is preferred by all governments but has to be traded off against the employment aim.

15. Notice that I do not model the influence of real exchange rate variations on output.

16. In this model the German economy is not hit by the European recession. This reflects the fact that the recession was felt later in Germany. Moreover, that shock could be subsumed under ε as well.

17. Since only monetary policy decides which solution is preferred, I have set $g^* = \bar{y}^{-*} = \xi \equiv 0$ to simplify the comparison. The same applies to the comparisons for the German government and the Bundesbank.

18. Thus while Germany's five big economic research institutes regarded a target range for M3 money supply of 6 to 8 percent as being more appropriate, the Bundesbank only set a target rate of 4.5 to 6.5 percent for 1993 (The Economist, July 31, 1993: 70).

19. To simplify the result, I assume that $\widetilde{gm} - g_c m_c = 0$.

7

Monetary Disintegration in the Former Soviet Union

7.1. Introduction

Many of the countries of the former Soviet Union (FSU) still exhibit high rates of money growth, while foreign trade has collapsed, privatization is slow, and state owned enterprises still account for a major share of GDP. This chapter studies the interaction among high inflation and the collapse of the trading system and the ruble zone to assess how currency and trade relations can be expected to be designed in the future.

Strikingly, the history of the nineteenth century in Europe seems to repeat partly in the former Soviet Union republics. The absence of a developed fiscal system has revived the seigniorage revenue motive for money creation. One also observes again the important influence of nationalistic feelings. The lessons from that early experience can be applied as well. Without the existence of a *single* central bank, no currency union is viable.

Recently, a large body of literature has developed which addresses the reason for the high rates of money creation. Building on similar experiences in developing and reforming countries in other parts of the world, as well as historical experiences in post-World War II Europe, it is argued that high rates of money creation are the result of a distributional struggle between interest groups (Alesina and Drazen 1991; Casella and Eichengreen 1996; Laban and Sturzenegger 1994). Large public deficits are monetized because fiscal reform, implying that public spending has to be cut while tax revenue has to be increased, finds no consensus. In this view, the main driving force for money creation is the fiscal needs of governments which, absent other sources of finance, has to rely on seigniorage to cover public expenditures. Other sources of finance cannot be agreed upon because the costs of stabilization are asymmetrically distributed. One interest group benefits from public spending while another group would have to bear the main burden from fiscal reform. This monetization of deficits had disastrous effects upon the working of the payments system in the FSU. The common payments system and the ruble zone broke down because of the different fiscal needs of the new independent states and as a consequence of the obvious free-rider problem created in a monetary union with competing monetary authorities (Lipton and Sachs 1992; Gros and Steinherr 1995). Moreover, different rates of money creation are ultimately incompatible with stable exchange rates. Thus different growth rates of money supply are one important reason for the collapse of the ruble zone and the dissolution of the trading system among the countries of the FSU.[1]

While many external observers are convinced that a common currency is not a preferable choice for the republics (Goldberg at al. 1994; Gros and Steinherr 1995; Hefeker 1995a; Willett and Al-Marhubi 1994), others yet point out the need of a common payments system to foster trade (see e.g. Williamson 1992). This view is based on the opinion that a revival of trade among these economies is highly desirable and of vital importance for income and the reform process. Normative analyses are hence concerned with different ways to resurrect the trading system, where one discussed transitional mechanism has been a payments union (Bofinger 1991b; Ethier 1992; Kenen 1991). Referring to experiences in post-World War II Europe, the European Payments Union is identified as a major contributing factor to the growth process, because it made rapid trade expansion possible (Eichengreen 1993b). Among other prominent proposals is a currency board (Lipton and Sachs 1992). For a comprehensive discussion of possible solutions, see Williamson (1992).

In this chapter I apply the positive political-economy perspective to the two interrelated problems of money creation and the exchange rate regime. While the reasons for excessive money creation are well established, the positive analysis of the choice of the exchange rate regime for economies in transition is less developed. Thus it is the aim of this chapter to analyze simultaneously the relation between distributional conflict in a country, giving rise to money creation and the collapse of fixed exchange rates, and the interests of the trading sector in that country. Given that stable exchange rates are important for international trade, the question is when and how the internal distributional conflicts can be solved to make stable exchange rates possible.

The discussion is organized as follows. I first discuss the budgetary problems of a transition economy, giving rise to a free-rider problem and competitive money creation in a monetary union. Sections 7.3 and 7.4 describe the ensuing collapse of the monetary union and the trading network in the FSU. The next section develops a stylized model to combine the problem of money creation and the different phases of the dissolution of the ruble zone. On this basis the likelihood of and the conditions for a new monetary arrangement are analyzed in Section 7.6. In the last part of the chapter, I suggest that at least some of the states of the former Soviet Union will finally return to a fixed exchange rate regime. It becomes also clear that support from the West might help not only to stabilize internally but to revive trade.

7.2. Fiscal Deficits and Money Creation

The source of the budgetary crisis in transition economies can be located in the old system of government revenue in centrally planned economies. Under old-style central planning the whole capital stock was owned and controlled by the central government and the surpluses of enterprises were thus fiscal revenue (for details, see Mc Kinnon 1991). With perestroika, however, this system of implicit taxation dissolved. As the effective ownership and control of enterprises passed from the central government to private farmers, managers, independent industrial cooperatives and local governments, the implicit tax base for the central government vanished. Moreover, if an enterprise had faced a shortage of credit for goods it needed to fulfill the plan under central planning, the state bank had automatically advanced the necessary credit at a zero or low rate of interest. This was the so-called soft-budget constraint. Problems arose when the monetary system continued to serve enterprises automatically after liberalization. Once enterprises began to make their own decisions they started to bid excessively for resources because they had no effective budget constraint. And as the future of many firms became uncertain, the time horizon of managers and workers shortened, inducing them to appropriate the firms' assets. Given the soft-budget constraint, managers granted excessive wages to workers, since many of the managements in the state owned enterprises felt more loyal to them than to the formal owner, the state (see Milesi-Feretti 1995a). Firms thus were no longer able to support government budgets from profits, but in contrast even relied on the government to cover rapidly increasing deficits. Governments went from taxing firms to subsidizing them and ran into budget deficits themselves.[2] Moreover, as newly independent republics struggled with the central government about political influence, thus bidding for the loyalties of enterprises, particularly in the military-industrial complex, they granted credits at negative real interest rates and established new banks which were generously refinanced by newly created central banks (Lipton and Sachs 1992).

These subsidies have, of course, distributional effects. State credits guarantee that directors of large enterprises retain their elite position in society as the patriarchs of their collectives and are able to secure a continuing flow of funds, given their close connection to policymakers. Further rent-defending interest groups are managers, workers and the inhabitants of towns where one enterprise is the economic base who all lose rents if market forces are left to force the enterprise into bankruptcy and closure (Hillman 1994). Yet, a compensation of these rent-defending interest is either not possible because the magnitude of payments cannot be assessed, the promise of compensation payments is not credible (see Dewatripont and Roland 1992), or simply because many of these activities are illegal. And while the state owned enterprises continuously depend on subsidies to support output and employment, the developing private sector has to finance those subsidies. It is obvious, though, that that sector is unwilling to pay taxes to support the old sector. Thus the government faces a dilemma. While a small private sector has not enough political influence to avoid being taxed, the tax revenue would be small as well. A large sector instead can probably mobilize enough political support to avoid being excessively taxed. Governments may then resort to finance subsidies by money creation. But then the implied monetary destabilization hurts the population at large as it redistributes income from households towards that small part of the population that is able to obtain huge amounts of cheap credits.

7.3. Leaving the Ruble Zone

In the Soviet Union monetary control was exercised by the State Bank, the Gosbank, which began increasingly to lose control over monetary policy in the republics. At the end of 1991, following the break up of the Soviet Union into 15 independent states, the Gosbank was replaced by 15 regional central banks. Although the central bank of Russia retained the sole right of printing money, all others had the ability to set interest rates and credit policies independently. The absence of control created a serious free-rider problem in which the individual states could expand credit to finance their budget deficits as deemed appropriate and share the costs of doing so with all the others (see Christensen 1994; Miller 1993).

The central bank of Russia, however, was the only of the 15 central banks which had the ability to print cash money, since all the printing presses were located in Russia (see Bofinger et al. 1993). The other republics were hence dependent on Russia's deliveries of cash money. As a result many started to print surrogate money, like coupons, or left the ruble zone altogether.[3] The republics remaining in the ruble zone, however, continued to grant ruble credits to their enterprises that could be used to pay resources in other republics. Thus states had a monetary system in which cash was independently printed and credits were extended in rubles (see Lipton and Sachs 1992; Gros and Steinherr 1995, for details).[4]

To prevent the spread of inflation among the republics, Russia introduced correspondent accounts in early 1992. All Russia related intra-republican payments had to be channeled through these accounts. The system required the registration of all transactions and could thus be used to control trade flows to avoid any surpluses with the republics. In July 1992 Russia decreed that these accounts had to be balanced, introducing factually bilateralism. Nevertheless, Russia granted the republics a certain limit of credit to help start the system. These credit limits were not taken too seriously and very soon exhausted. One reason was certainly that the Russian government was under pressure from its exporters to grant these credits to foster exports to the republics (Eichengreen 1993b). Since many of the large enterprises relied heavily on inter-republican trade they objected to increases in the costs of trade and the anticipated reductions in exports of their products (Goldberg et al. 1994).

Given this arrangement, the republics' initial ability to create credit was due to Russia's political decision to give them this ability. The free-rider problem was thus politically accepted by Russia and could have been avoided. The republics on the other hand continuously exhausted their credit lines, since there was no possibility to use surpluses gained in trade with one republic to buy goods from another republic. Hence every republic took care not to acquire surpluses in intra-FSU trade. Given this framework, enterprises preferred direct barter amongst themselves where possible to the indirect barter via the payments system (Hillman 1994).

Since the introduction of correspondent accounts and the control of ruble deliveries finally deprived the republics of the ability to create rubles, they had to choose between breaking away from the ruble zone, being able to conduct an independent monetary policy, and the implied loss of cheap credits from the Russian central bank and oil subsidies, which were tied to membership in the ruble zone. Most of the former Soviet republics hesitated to introduce convertible currencies because they expected to have to pay a higher price for Russian energy supply and to have no longer access to Russian credits at negative real interest rates (Gros and Steinherr 1995). For details on redistribution, see Christensen (1994, Appendix III).

7.4. The Contraction of FSU-Trade

Before the dissolution of the Soviet Union 70 to 75 percent of the trade was intra-SU trade, resulting from the high specialization of the republics (Christensen 1994). Since the break up of the Soviet Union, however, trade has spiralled downward.[5] Between 1990 and 1993 trade with third countries declined to less than one half, whereas intra-republican trade declined even more. However, each republic's trade with Russia fell less than trade with each other (Michalopoulos and Tarr 1994). While one reason for the decline in trade is surely the collapse in production (output has fallen by 10 percent in 1991, and another 20 percent in 1992 in the former Soviet Union), trade has declined even more (Eichengreen 1993b).

Besides the general output collapse, a magnifying factor in the collapse of trade was that after the dissolution of the Soviet Union the new independent states imposed taxes and quantitative restrictions on their exports and negotiated bilateral trade arrangements in which exports should balance imports.[6] This was deemed necessary because the different speeds of price liberalization, especially in 1991, gave incentives to widespread arbitrage. Shortages in food, consumer goods, energy and industrial materials led governments to impose strict export controls.

Yet another contributor to the collapse of trade has been the variability of exchange rates. The large under- and overvaluations of the currencies have created political pressures. While overvaluation of the home currency implies import pressure from abroad, undervaluation is opposed because it is feared that foreigners buy out the home country (Havrylyshyn 1994). Closely connected with the variability of exchange rates is the impact of the absence of a common payments systems and convertibility of payments among the new currencies. Under bilateralism no possibility of multilateral clearing exists. This means that surpluses acquired with one trading partner cannot be used to pay for deficits with others. Therefore, trade with any single partner is restricted to the respective smaller part of supply of exports and demand for imports. The volume of trade falls since countries are unwilling to grant credits to each other. Especially countries which are likely to be structural creditors, like those possessing minerals and oil, are unwilling to grant credits since there is almost no chance that they will ever receive payment for their credits (Eichengreen 1993b).

7.5. Modeling the End of the Ruble Zone

In this section, I present a simple stylized model which should capture the main traits of the development in the FSU. It can obviously not do justice to all single republics nor capture all aspects which had an influence. It is developed to follow the developments in the ruble zone and to explain its collapse. This framework will then be used in the next section to assess the likelihood of and the conditions for new monetary arrangements for the republics of the FSU.

The model is a one-country model with two sectors that are caught in a distributional struggle. It is again a variant of the basic model developed in Chapter 2. It contains two sectors, whose output aim, for analytical tractability, enters the politician's objective function only linearly. The two sectors are the sector of the state owned enterprises and a developing sector of private enterprises. The output of the sector with state owned enterprises (indexed S) is given as

(7.1) $$y_S = \gamma g + \overline{y}_E \left[1 - T_E - \sigma_E^2(e_E) \right].$$

Output in that sector is determined by two sources. Part of the production in this sector is sold domestically and can be additionally stimulated through government subsidies g.[7] The second part of the production is exposed to trade with other former centrally planned economies. Trade with the West is not modeled because it is assumed for simplicity that the products produced in this sector are not competitive in the West. This part of the output depends positively on an exogenous foreign demand component $\overline{y}_E$ reflecting, for example, the size of or the income in that country. The output is, however, negatively affected by trading costs T and by currency variability. Whenever the exchange regime is a flexible one, traders incur costs from currency fluctuation, which affects profits and output in the sector negatively, like in Chapter 4. This reflects transaction costs, and in addition to the argumentation in Chapter 4, the fact that managers in the FSU are not used to calculating with changing currency values. Moreover, short-term instruments to cover currency risk, like hedging, are not available. Hence, this sector benefits from exchange rate stability with FSU republics.

The same is true for the private, or market oriented, part of the economy (indexed P). That sector, producing goods which are marketable in the West, trades with market economies only instead of FSU partners. Its production is internationally competitive. Thus

(7.2) $$y_P = -\gamma t + \overline{y}_W \left[1 - T_W - \sigma_W^2(e_W) \right].$$

However, the reforming sector might be subject to taxation t which affects profits and employment negatively. Exchange rate variability affects trade in the private sector as well.

The government's budget constraint is given as

(7.3) $$g + \overline{g} = t + S_E + S_W + \beta \pi.$$

Subsidies to state owned enterprises g and exogenous expenditures $\overline{g}$ (reflecting for example the costs of the operation of the government) have to be financed through taxation t on the private sector, through revenue from inflation $\beta \pi$, and through subsidies S from the trading partners in the FSU and the West.[8] Since S_E captures the subsidized credits and oil imports for the republics given by Russia, it is negative for Russia.

Assuming that relative purchasing power parity holds for floating exchange rates, changes in the exchange rate are a function of the difference in the rates of inflation between the countries.[9] Therefore,

(7.4) $e_E = \pi - \pi_E$ and $e_w = \pi - \pi_w$,

where π_w is set to zero throughout the analysis. The assumption is hence in this chapter that money supply increases directly translate into inflation.[10]

The costs for trade with the two different trading partners $T_{E,w}$ are a function of an exogenous part $\bar{\tau}$, reflecting the pure trading costs, given through the geographical distance, and a policy variable τ which reflects politically set trading barriers. Those could be tariffs set by the respective trading partner or reflect an export or import tax of the own government (which can also be negative).[11] Thus

(7.5) $T_E = \bar{\tau}_E + \tau_E$ and $T_w = \bar{\tau}_w + \tau_w$.

Policy decisions of the government are determined by its goal to maximize political support since any government is required to have political support to stay in office (see Hillman et al. 1993). This political support is provided by the two sectors, where their support is a function of the deviations of current output from a target level in that sector. Higher output implies higher profits and, most importantly, higher employment.[12] Thus governments, in a situation of unemployment, have an incentive to increase output in the sector with state owned enterprises to pay subsidies, and on the other hand to avoid taxation of the privatized sector. On the other hand, the public is averse to inflation which rises when subsidies are financed through inflation (the target rate of inflation is set to zero). Political support for the government is given as

$$
\begin{aligned}
V^i = &\ \delta_s \gamma g + \varphi_s \bar{y}_E \left[1 - T_E - \sigma_E^2 (e_E) \right] \\
&- \delta_P \gamma t + \varphi_P \bar{y}_w \left[1 - T_w - \sigma_w^2 (e_w) \right] \qquad i = R, I \\
&- \frac{\omega}{2} \pi^2 .
\end{aligned}
$$
(7.6)

In what follows a difference will be made between the decisions of the Russian government (R) and those of the governments in the newly independent states (I) where necessary. δ and φ are the political weights the domestic and trade exposed component in each of the two sectors have. It depends on the size of the component, hence a higher degree of openness of an economy raises the political influence of the trading sectors. A sector's influence, however, might also be overproportional because of its (strategic) importance, like agriculture or the military, because there are close personal links between managers and the government, or simply because that sector is better able to overcome the collective action problem to organize itself. Political support for the government increases with output in the two sectors and decreases with inflation where ω is the weight of inflation aversion.

It is obvious (by using (7.3) in (7.6)) that both sectors favor inflationary financing instead of losing subsidies or having to finance them via taxation respectively. The government balances the sectors' interests to maximize political support and has thus to revise its decision when the structure of the economy changes, as can be expected during the transition to a market economy. Governments have to obey the political support constraint at all points in time but especially before elections.[13]

Competitive Money Creation in the FSU

This subsection describes the brief period where already 15 central banks existed but before Russia introduced the correspondent accounts. It provides the basis for the decision of the Russian government to introduce binding correspondent accounts described in the next subsection. The situation where the republics compete in money creation is characterized by fixed exchange rates between the republics. Imported inflation from other republics is the difference between imported and exported inflation, $\pi_E - \pi$. In this case the trade barriers among the republics are zero and the Russian government supports the other republics by, for example, delivering artificially cheap mineral products. For the Russian republic, of course, this effect enters negatively. The competitive case (indexed C) is characterized by the attempt to export more inflation than to import it. This is the free-rider problem extensively discussed in the literature (see e.g. Miller 1993). It becomes more important as the degree of trade integration with the trading partner in the currency union increases. This is portrayed as $\varphi_s(\pi_E - \pi)$.

The government's decision problem is

$$
\begin{aligned}
\max_\pi V_C^i = &\ \delta_s \gamma \left(S_E - \overline{g} + t + \beta\pi \right) + \varphi_s \overline{y_E} \left(1 - \overline{\tau_E} \right) \\
&- \delta_P \gamma \left(g + \overline{g} - S_E - \beta\pi \right) + \varphi_P \overline{y_w} \left[1 - T_w - \sigma_w^2 (e_w) \right] \\
&- \frac{\omega}{2} \left\{ \pi(1 - \varphi_s) + \varphi_s \pi_E \right\}^2 .
\end{aligned}
$$
(7.7)

Maximization yields the politically optimal rate of inflation as a reaction to the other republics' rate of inflation

(7.8)
$$\pi = \frac{a - \omega b \varphi_s \pi_E}{\omega b^2}$$

where $a \equiv \gamma\beta(\delta_s + \delta_P) > 0$ and $b \equiv (1 - \varphi_s) > 0$.

This reflects the interests of both sectors that favor inflation because the state owned enterprises receive subsidies via inflation and the private sector prefers inflation to taxation which is supported by the chance to export part of the domestic inflation.

Political support for the government in this situation is given as, by using (7.8) in (7.7),

(7.9)
$$\begin{aligned}
. V_c^i &= \gamma\left(S_E - \overline{g}\right)\left(\delta_s + \delta_P\right) + \delta_s \gamma t - \delta_P \gamma g \\
&\quad + \varphi_s \overline{y_E}\left(1 - \overline{\tau_E}\right) + \varphi_P \overline{y_w}\left[1 - T_w - \sigma_w^2(e_w)\right] \\
&\quad + \frac{a}{b}\left(\frac{a}{2\omega b} - \varphi_s \pi_E\right).
\end{aligned}$$

Political support is positively dependent on the exogenous trade components. The state owned enterprises support taxes while the private sector is opposed to subsidies which reflects the distributional struggle between the two sectors. The last term captures the opposing influences of being able to increase inflation to solve the distributional struggle between the two sectors, and on the other hand, the aversion against imported inflation.

The Introduction of Correspondent Accounts

As described, in 1992 Russia introduced correspondent accounts and restricted cash deliveries to stop the free-rider behavior among the republics. Assuming that Russia can directly control the rate of inflation in the ruble zone in this situation, the government's problem is

(7.10)
$$\begin{aligned}
\max_\pi V_{CA}^R &= \delta_s \gamma\left(-S_E - \overline{g} + t + \beta\pi\right) + \varphi_s \overline{y_E}\left(1 - \overline{\tau_E}\right) \\
&\quad - \delta_P \gamma\left(g + \overline{g} + S_E - \beta\pi\right) + \varphi_P \overline{y_w}\left[1 - T_w - \sigma_w^2(e_w)\right] \\
&\quad - \frac{\omega}{2}\pi^2.
\end{aligned}$$

Hence Russia is able to control the rate of inflation in the ruble zone but does not change the amount of redistribution paid, nor does it erect trade barriers in this case. Then the optimal rate of inflation chosen is given as

(7.11)
$$\pi = \frac{a}{\omega}.$$

Given this rate of inflation, political support for the Russian government is the following

(7.12)
$$V_{CA}^{R} = +\delta_s \gamma t - \delta_P \gamma g - \gamma \left(S_E + \overline{g}\right)\left(\delta_s + \delta_P\right)$$
$$+\varphi_s \overline{y_E}\left(1 - \overline{\tau_E}\right) + \varphi_P \overline{y_W}\left[1 - T_W - \sigma_W^2\left(e_W\right)\right]$$
$$+\frac{a^2}{2\omega}.$$

The decision to introduce the correspondent accounts can be reproduced easily. The Russian government will choose to introduce correspondent accounts if $V_{CA}^{R} - V_{C}^{R} \geq 0$. This is the case if

(7.13)
$$\frac{a^2}{2\omega} + \frac{a\varphi_s \pi_E}{b} \geq \frac{a^2}{2\omega b^2}.$$

Whenever the inflation that is imported from abroad π_E is sufficiently large, this negative influence overcompensates the utility from being able to share the costs of inflationary budget financing, which is captured by the term on the right hand side. Then, however, the Russian government can raise its domestic political support by introducing the correspondent accounts.

The End of the Ruble Zone

The situation under the existence of correspondent accounts for the smaller republics, however, is that they have to take the rate of inflation as given, without receiving the revenues from it because those accrue to Russia. For those governments political support is given as

(7.14)
$$V_{CA}^{I} = \left(\delta_s + \delta_P\right)\gamma\left(S_E - \overline{g}\right) + \delta_s \gamma t - \delta_P \gamma g$$
$$+\varphi_s \overline{y_E}\left(1 - \overline{\tau_E}\right) + \varphi_P \overline{y_W}\left[1 - T_W - \sigma_W^2\left(e_W\right)\right] - \overline{\pi}^2.$$

where $\bar{\pi}$ is the rate of inflation set by Russia.

To explain the collapse of the ruble zone, the situation after leaving the ruble zone has to be compared to that under correspondent accounts. After leaving the ruble zone and the introduction of an own currency the government's problem is

(7.15)
$$\max_{\pi} V_N^I = \delta_s \left[\overline{y_s} + \gamma \left(t - \bar{g} + \beta\pi \right) \right] + \varphi_s \overline{y_E} \left[1 - T_E - \sigma_E^2 \left(e_E \right) \right]$$
$$+ \delta_P \left[\overline{y_P} - \gamma \left(g + \bar{g} - \beta\pi \right) \right] + \varphi_P \overline{y_W} \left[1 - T_W - \sigma_W^2 \left(e_W \right) \right]$$
$$- \frac{\omega}{2} \pi^2 + \lambda N.$$

where the index N captures the influences of nationalism.

Now trade with Russia is subject to exchange rate fluctuations and presumably to artificial trade barriers. As described in Section 7.4, exchange rate variations often prompted trade barriers. Moreover, the republics that decide to leave the ruble zone have no longer financial support from the Russian government. This source of financing subsidies and other expenditures is lost. I add, however, a positive dummy λN which captures nationalistic feelings and the pride of having an own money. This seems to have been important for some of the smaller republics (Havrylyshyn and Williamson 1991).

Maximization of (7.15) yields the politically optimal rate of inflation for this case as

(7.16)
$$\pi = \frac{a}{\omega}.$$

Political support for the government in the smaller republic becomes

(7.17)
$$V_N^I = \delta_s \overline{y_s} + \delta_P \overline{y_P} - \gamma \bar{g} \left(\delta_s + \delta_P \right)$$
$$+ \delta_s \gamma t - \delta_P \gamma g + \varphi_s \overline{y_E} \left[1 - T_E - \sigma_E^2 \left(e_E \right) \right]$$
$$+ \varphi_P \overline{y_W} \left[1 - T_W - \sigma_W^2 \left(e_W \right) \right] + \frac{a^2}{2\omega} + \lambda N.$$

The decision to move towards an own money and to leave the ruble zone is determined by the difference between the two levels of public support for the respective situation. The government will decide to accept a loss of subsidies and exchange rate stability *vis-à-vis* the trading partner Russia if the gain from an independent monetary policy is larger. This is the case if $V_N^I - V_{CA}^I \geq 0$, which is equivalent to

$$(7.18) \qquad \frac{a^2}{2\omega} + \frac{\omega}{2}\overline{\pi} + \lambda N \geq \gamma S_E \left(\delta_s + \delta_P \right) + \varphi_s \overline{y_E} \left[\tau_E + \sigma_E^2 \left(e_E \right) \right]$$

When assessing the benefits from nationalism, the government has to take into account that the trade policy of Russia might change towards protectionism and that flexible exchange rates have costs. In addition, the loss of subsidies from Russia will affect both sectors negatively. The state owned enterprises lose direct subsidies and the private sector will have to pay a higher price in terms of higher taxes or higher inflation. The gain from setting the own rate of inflation independently, receiving thus the revenue from it, and the aversion to accept Russia's rate of inflation must thus be at least as high as lost subsidies and the loses from trade barriers and exchange rate variability.

If the preferred rate of inflation to finance the sectors is considerably higher than the rate set by Russia, a republic might leave the ruble zone to be able to set a higher independent rate of inflation. Other republics, whose financing need is not as large, or which have a better tax structure, might leave to avoid the inflation spill-overs from Russia because their preferred rate is lower. Examples are the Ukraine where the rate of inflation after leaving the ruble zone has increased, or most other republics where inflation rates fell (see Gros and Steinherr 1995). Hence not only the strong feeling of nationalism might drive countries out of the ruble zone, although this effect is likely to have been pivotal in some cases.

7.6. Monetary Reintegration Among the Republics?

The dissolution of the ruble zone and the turn to bilateralism have seriously undermined the trade connection. Since payments have not been convertible, the result has been inefficient bilateralism (Eichengreen 1993). To revive trade with the other republics, some authors have suggested that the states of the former Soviet Union create a payments union among themselves (Bofinger 1991b; Kenen 1991). On the other hand, especially more recently, it has been argued that many countries will in the future trade more with the Western economies and some adjustments in this direction are already made (Gros and Steinherr 1995; Havrylyshyn 1994). Given that stable currency relations are beneficial to trade, the obvious alternative would be to try to fix the exchange rate *vis-à-vis* some Western economy. The Estonian currency board for example is based on the DM and could be a model for this solution. Both possible integration strategies are compared in this section.

Monetary reintegration presupposes that the FSU republics are ultimately able to solve their distributional conflict and compromise on economic stabilization. To achieve this a restructuring of the economy towards enlargement of the private sector is likely to be necessary. This will on the one hand reduce the need for subsidies and, *ceteris paribus*, reduce the budget deficit. On the other hand it will enlarge the tax base as the taxable sector becomes larger. Taxation will not be rejected if the sector values trade and exchange rate stability higher than ongoing destabilization. In terms of this model, this also shifts the trade orientation towards the West. The policy change would probably be accompanied by a change in the political system that reduces the influence of the state owned enterprises, reducing thereby as well the subsidies going to that sector. As democracy strengthens, one can expect that the inflation aversion of the general public becomes more important.

Reintegration with the Republics of the Former Soviet Union

If the republics should realize that stable exchange rates are conducive to their economic development and are able to influence the political process to such a policy, they have to decide whether to peg to the Russian currency. The subsidized deliveries of oil and other raw products might be one reason to reintegrate with Russia.[14] Russia in contrast is probably not willing to resume payments in the former order of magnitude. Nevertheless, for the case of reintegration with the FSU republics (indexed S) subsidies could again be part of such an arrangement. For this analysis, I assume a return to free trade. Hence the situation would be like that under the correspondent accounts. It would be

$$V_s^R = \delta_s \gamma t - \delta_P \gamma g - \gamma \left(S_E + \overline{g} \right) \left(\delta_s + \delta_P \right)$$

(7.12')
$$+ \varphi_s \overline{y}_E \left(1 - \overline{\tau}_E \right) + \varphi_P \overline{y}_w \left[1 - T_w - \sigma_w^2 \left(e_w \right) \right]$$

$$+ \frac{a^2}{2\omega}$$

for Russia, and for the republics it would respectively be

$$V_s^I = \gamma\left(S_E - \overline{g}\right)\left(\delta_s + \delta_P\right) + \delta_s \gamma t - \delta_P \gamma g$$

(7.14')
$$+ \varphi_s \overline{y}_E\left(1 - \overline{\tau}_E\right) + \varphi_P \overline{y}_W\left[1 - T_W - \sigma_W^2\left(e_W\right)\right]$$

$$-\frac{\omega}{2}\overline{\pi}^{-2}.$$

The decision to reenter a ruble zone implies for Russia $V_s^R - V_N^R \geq 0$. That is the case if

(7.19)
$$\varphi_s \overline{y}_E\left[\tau_E + \sigma_E^2\left(e_E\right)\right] \geq \gamma S_E\left(\delta_s + \delta_P\right) + \lambda N$$

while for the republics it implies that $V_s^I - V_N^I \geq 0$, or

(7.20)
$$\gamma S_E\left(\delta_s + \delta_P\right) + \varphi_s \overline{y}_E\left[\tau_E + \sigma_E^2\left(e_E\right)\right] \geq \frac{a^2}{2\omega} + \frac{\omega}{2}\overline{\pi}^{-2} + \lambda N.$$

Even if nationalism is not important for Russia ($N = 0$), the redistributive term (S_E) is negative because it would have to pay subsidies, only the effects of currency stability and free trade enter positively. Whether the condition is fulfilled depends ultimately on the subsidies which are involved with such an arrangement, implying that they would probably have to be considerably lower than before the collapse of the ruble zone to make reintegration attractive for Russia. For the republics, reversing (7.18), the condition (7.20) shows that the rate of inflation set by Russia ($\overline{\pi}$) is pivotal in their decision. It must not be too high. Thus, not only must the own desire to achieve output stabilization with the help of inflation disappear but must this incentive fall in Russia, making $\overline{\pi}$ sufficiently small. The amount of redistribution is valued positively but is likely to be smaller than before. Subsidies and the negative effects from currency variability must, however, overcompensate the benefits of independent monetary policy. And, of course, the nationalistic aim must not be too large.

Monetary Integration with the West

The other possible trade partner the government could choose to peg to is a subset of Western economies, as the Baltic states did. If the states of the former Soviet Union want to initiate a process of economic integration with the West, raise external trade, and attract foreign investment, they must guarantee political and economic stability. Reducing uncertainties about the exchange rate might be helpful as well. Under the assumption that those republics are entitled to receive some funds from the West instead of payments from Russia, which could be imagined as funds from the International Monetary Fund to stabilize the currency or from the European Union, that no trade barriers exist, and that the exchange rate with the West is constant, the political support function is

$$
\begin{aligned}
V_B^i = \delta_s\left[\overline{y_s} + \gamma\left(t - \overline{g} + S_w\right)\right] + \varphi_s \overline{y_E}\left[1 - T_E - \sigma_E^2\left(e_E\right)\right] \\
+ \delta_P\left[\overline{y_P} - \gamma\left(g + \overline{g} - S_w\right)\right] + \varphi_P \overline{y_w}\left(1 - \overline{\tau_w}\right).
\end{aligned}
$$

(7.21)

Comparing nationalism (7.17) and West integration (7.21) shows that the latter will be chosen if $V_B^i - V_N^i \geq 0$. Thus the following must hold:

(7.22) $\gamma S_w\left(\delta_s + \delta_P\right) + \varphi_P \overline{y_w}\left[\tau_w + \sigma_w^2\left(e_w\right)\right] \geq \dfrac{a^2}{2\omega} + \lambda N.$

For this decision, the size of a possible redistribution form the West is important. This condition, unlike before, can be expected to apply to Russia as well. While in the alternative scenario, Russia would be expected to pay such subsidies, it could be expected to be net-receiver of funds with Western integration. A second beneficial influence is that inflation is lower in this case when compared to a monetary integration with other former FSU republics. But again, the output stabilizing effect of monetary autonomy is lost. Finally, the pegging to a Western currency might entail smaller costs of losing the national symbol for the smaller republics, because the adversity to Russia might be large, whereas pegging to the West might not entail this political adversity. The different degrees of nationalism are not modeled here, however.

A Comparison of the Integration Strategies

Presuming that the government decides that integration is beneficial, the question is with whom to integrate. The standard analysis of customs unions shows that the expected gains are larger the less the degree of protection exercised by the union, the larger the size of the union, and the more similar the size and structure of countries joining the union are. Among countries with a comparable level of development, the geographical distribution of trade is to a considerable degree influenced by the so-called gravitational factors: distance, cultural affinity, and the size of the different markets. These factors suggest that the EU is likely to become the dominant trading partner for the European republics of the FSU. The Baltic states are likely to trade primarily with Europe, while the Central Asian republics can be expected to continue to trade extensively with Russia because of their lower level of development and their geographical position. The Ukraine, Belorussia and the Transcaucasian republics are intermediate cases. Ukraine and Belorussia have an industry structure that suggests the possibility of extensive trade with the West, but geography and culture suggest ties with Russia (Gros and Steinherr 1995).

Comparing utility levels achieved with West and East integration respectively, that is (7.21) and (7.19), implies that West integration would be chosen if

$$
(7.23) \quad
\begin{aligned}
&\gamma\left(S_w + S_E\right)\left(\delta_s + \delta_P\right) + \varphi_P \overline{y_w}\left[\tau_w + \sigma_w^2\left(e_w\right)\right] \\
&\geq \frac{a}{2\omega}^2 + \varphi_s \overline{y_E}\left[\tau_E + \sigma_E^2\left(e_E\right)\right] - \lambda N.
\end{aligned}
$$

for Russia.

For the other republics (7.20) and (7.21) compared yields as condition

$$
(7.24) \quad
\begin{aligned}
&\gamma\left(S_w - S_E\right)\left(\delta_s + \delta_P\right) + \varphi_P \overline{y_w}\left[\tau_w + \sigma_w^2\left(e_w\right)\right] + \frac{\omega}{2}\pi^{-2} \\
&\geq \varphi_s \overline{y_E}\left[\tau_E + \sigma_E^2\left(e_E\right)\right]
\end{aligned}
$$

Thus integration with the West would be sought if the redistribution to be obtained from the West is higher than in the alternative case and if the importance of trade with the West for the economy increases. Notice that the redistribution to be expected from Russia is likely to be smaller than before the collapse of the ruble zone. For Russia, to save this amount enters the condition (7.23) positively. On the other side, if trade with the FSU is more important and the inflation is still needed to stabilize output, West integration is less likely.

Monetary stabilization does in any case imply for the small republics to give up monetary policy and the revenues from inflation. This presupposes that another source of finance can be found and that the distributional struggle between the domestic interest groups can be solved. For Russia, only Western integration implies giving up monetary autonomy. On the other hand, reintegration with FSU republics would incur subsidies to make this attractive for the republics. Thus both FSU partners must rely heavily on each other, either for political or economic reasons, to make reintegration worthwhile. [15]

7.7. Conclusion

One important factor whether stabilization can be successful in the economies in transition is whether they are able to stabilize their budgets. This can be achieved in several ways. First of all, expenditures have to be reduced. This requires to stop subsidizing monopolistic enterprises. This sector, however, can be expected to shrink anyway, but the speed can of course be accelerated when other factors for political support for a government increase. The second way is to increase the government funding by establishing a tax structure. This takes time but will ultimately develop. A third source is external support. Casella and Eichengreen (1996) argue in this regard that external help might be important to support the end of the war of attrition described in this chapter. They also point out that timing is important and that waiting too long may further de-stabilize and postpone reforms.

The Baltic states are examples of the influence of external funding. Estonia's stabilization program for example was made possible by large gold funds which were returned from the Bank of England to Estonia after independence. Moreover, the Baltic states are supported by the Scandinavian states and the West in general. Extending this help to other states as well might accelerate stabilization and return to trade in the transition economies. In the same manner, redistribution from Russia connected with reintegration might achieve exactly this for some of the Asian republics whose decision to seek some new form of integration with the large trading partner reflects the necessity of funding from abroad.

It seems likely that many of the states will, sooner or later, decide to adopt fixed exchange rates, joining the trend in many Western economies. The evidence is that at least trade-dependent economies prefer fixed rates. The trading pattern and thus the geographical position of a country will hence ultimately determine to which country the independent republics will peg. In as far as trade with Western economies dominates, it is likely that some republics follow the Baltic example and peg to a Western currency. For the other republics, however, a reintegration with Russia seems possible.

Notes

1. The seigniorage need of countries is seen as one important reason for the choice of exchange rate regimes (see Canzoneri and Rogers 1990; Grilli 1989). As argued in Chapter 2, this is irrelevant for most Western economies although it apparently influences the choice of the countries considered in this chapter.

2. Notice that privatization loosens the relationship between state and enterprise. Private enterprises are less able to exert the same pressure for subsidies as when the state itself is owner of the enterprise. There might even be pressures not to subsidize a privatized firm, especially when the firm is foreign owned or when a foreign firm is a significant joint venture partner. A large scale privatization will hence be conducive to stabilization policies.

3. In June 1992, Estonia left the ruble zone and was followed by Lithuania, Latvia and Ukraine later that year, and the Kyrgyz Republic in 1993. For a chronology of the introduction of new currencies in the republics, see Garber and Spencer (1994).

4. Gros and Steinherr (1995) argue that, because credit had ultimately to be converted into cash to pay for wages and products, the control of cash was enough to control total money creation. Although the separation between and cash and credit was not perfect they compare this to a currency board, with the ruble as the reserve currency.

5. Notice that gravity models would predict such a fall in intra-FSU trade. For a discussion of gravity models and the trade pattern before and after the Soviet Union's dissolution, see Gros and Steinherr (1995) and Havrylyshyn (1994).

6. The same behavior could be observed by the states of the dissolving Austro-Hungarian Empire after World War I (Dornbusch 1992; Garber and Spencer 1994).

7. This neglects the influence of capital endowment in the two sectors. Investment in the private sector may be low, but foreigners could contribute to that (Hillman et al. 1993), while the resources of the state owned enterprises might be distributed to workers and managers. Then the capital stock will be depleted (Milesi-Feretti 1995a).

8. By setting β constant, I disregard the dynamics of high inflation. Inflation from the financing of budget deficits may be accelerated for a number of reasons. The delay in collecting taxes reduces the real tax revenues (Keynes 1923) and the unwillingness of the public to hold the inflationary currency and its resort to foreign money require an ever higher rate of inflation to finance a given deficit. The dynamics of high inflations are analyzed in detail by Dornbusch et al. (1990).

9. Assuming purchasing power parity is an obvious simplification. Many of the republics were and still are characterized by massive real overvaluation because exchange rates do not adjust according to inflation differentials.

10. In terms of the basic model in Chapter 2 this means that $\chi = \kappa = \phi = 1$.

11. I disregard the influence an export tax/subsidy or import tariff/subsidy has on the government's budget.

12. As long as employment can be kept high, social security and unemployment payments, which are also an important factor in the government's budget, will not reach an extraordinary magnitude. Those payments are hence disregarded in this analysis.

13. The model excludes ideological or partisan aims of the government. It also disregards different degrees of democratization of a society.

14. Belorussia is one example where the external help from Russia is combined with discussion of a currency union between the two countries. While Belorussia requests the revival of external support from Russia, Russia is reluctant to resume its payments.

15. Assuming that Russia might have a hegemonic political interest, nationalism λN could become negative for Russia.

8

Conclusion

This study asked whether changes in exchange rate regimes can be explained and predicted. To answer this question political economy theory has been used because the normative theory is inadequate for this task. Many of the criteria developed there are not fulfilled by countries which form a currency area, and most of the existing currency areas in the form of nation states are not optimum currency areas as defined by that theory. Where some of those criteria are fulfilled, there still is the problem that the theoretical foundation is not convincing. The assumption of welfare-maximizing governments is just too far away from reality. Thus, theories based on that assumption are necessarily incomplete and lead to wrong predictions.

With the help of political economy theory, especially the interest group approach, this book argued that the influence of those groups can to a large extent explain the choice of fixed exchange rates as opposed to flexible exchange rates. I argue that exchange rate variability adversely affects the output and the profits of the tradable goods producing industries. Uncertainty about future prices leads that sector to produce less, trade less, and hence lowers its output. Thus profits and profit opportunities are reduced and employment is lowered. Given that factors of production are often immobile, at least in the short-run, labor and capital in that sector unite and exert political pressure on policymakers to adopt fixed exchange rates. Thus, fixed exchange rates will be chosen if the political influence of that sector is strong enough.

The choice of the exchange rate regime can therefore be explained to a large degree by the influence of the tradables sector. But why do states time and again suspend their fixed exchange rate? The shift in the regime can be explained by exogenous shocks that either force the government to expand the money supply to be able to finance increased government spending, which was the case in the nineteenth-century Europe and is repeated in the countries of the former Soviet Union. Since the tax system in most of the Western economies is better developed, the seigniorage-raising motive for money creation is less important there. Hence the second reason for suspending the fixed exchange rate can be seen in the output stabilizing function of money. Given that raising the money supply can at least temporarily raise output and production in the economy, the government is tempted to increase the money supply when negative output shocks occur. Hence, exchange rate regime choice is not necessarily driven by considerations about exchange rate policy *per se* as optimum currency area theory would suggest, but by the implications it has for monetary policy. External shocks may bring down fixed exchange rates not because countries want to devalue, but rather because they want to have the possibility to reflate their economies.

Output shocks, however, have to be asymmetrically distributed across countries since they otherwise can raise their domestic money supplies in a coordinated way without undermining the viability of the fixed exchange rate regime. Since European economies are characterized by increasingly similar production structures and intra-industrial trade rather than inter-industry trade, asymmetric shocks in the tradables sector are likely to occur less frequently. Thus, asymmetric exogenous shocks are likely to be shocks to the non-tradables sector.[1] Since for these industries exchange rate stability is of less influence for their output, that sector will demand a monetary stabilization policy to counter an adverse output effect on that sector. If the shock is strong enough, and the political influence of that sector is large enough, the government will then temporarily suspend the fixed exchange rate commitment and resort to monetary stabilization policy.

These finding are partly compatible with the suggestions of optimum currency area theory. I argue, as Mc Kinnon (1963) suggested, that countries with a large tradables sector will choose fixed exchange rates. Moreover, recent developments in the theory of exchange rate regimes suggest that fixed exchange rates are temporarily suspended when large external financing needs arise (Bordo and Kydland 1995; De Kock and Grilli 1993). Both approaches have in common that they assume a welfare-maximizing government whose only consideration is to maximize overall welfare for the economy. This is unconvincing, because governments are usually not such welfare-maximizing benevolent dictators. Rather they, as everybody else in the economy, tend to maximize their own welfare which is dependent on political support and the chance of staying in office. To reach this aim they depend on interest groups' support and thus distributional effects become important in the policymaker's decision if interest groups have opposing aims.

Thus normative economic theory cannot adequately describe the behavior of governments. Additionally each of the two approaches focuses only on one aspect of the cycle which is the subject of this study. While optimum currency area theory only asks what regime is appropriate for a given economy, it disregards changes in the regime and especially credibility issue which may arise, because it basically equates fixed exchange rates to monetary union. The second approach focuses instead only on the collapse of the fixed exchange rate, taking the choice of fixed rates as given. There the choice is concerned with credibility of monetary stability and requires that the suspension of the peg is only temporary and the return to the fixed rate is predictable by the public. This is, of course, a highly dubious assumption. Governments usually do not adopt a floating rate and announce the exact time when they return to the fixed rate.

Thus both approaches have important limitations. It has been the aim of this study to develop a political-economic framework that encompasses the choice and collapse of fixed exchange rate regimes. It could be shown that the interests of important economic actors that determined the choice and collapse of fixed exchange rates are more or less stable over time. However, institutional changes, as in the tax system, and with regard to capital mobility and the political system, explain particular episodes in the history of attempts to reach monetary integration.

8.1. Monetary Integration and Disintegration in Europe

In 1923, Karl Helfferich wrote "Der Gedanke einer Weltmünzeinheit ist fast so alt, wie die Verschiedenheit der Münzverfassungen der einzelnen Länder" (1923: 135).[2] This shows that the nineteenth century, with which this study starts, is not the beginning of attempts of monetary integration. It is different, however, in another aspect. Come the industrial revolution, the interest of the trading sectors became an important political factor to recognize. Those interests sided with the still important political hegemony interests of some states, like France or Prussia. Those who defended monetary autonomy instead were the ones who financed themselves by money creation, the single states that wanted to preserve their independent instruments, and the ones who profited from monetary confusion, namely the banks.

Given monetary sovereignty for single members in the different monetary unions, competitive money creation was the result. Only monetary centralization was able to overcome this incentive. The other important factor for the stability of the common monetary system was the occurrence of shocks which forced states like Italy and Greece to suspend their peg to be able to seigniorage-finance their budgets. Thus a monetary union is only viable with one monetary institution and if asymmetric shocks are not too strong, a lesson that applies to the case of the former Soviet Union as well.

Money creation for revenue purposes and competitive money creation are behind monetary disintegration in the former Soviet Union republics as well. The support of the monopolistic sectors requires spending which can only be financed through seigniorage, absent a well developed tax system. States broke away from Russia either to avoid being flooded with other republics' money or to be able to increase their own seigniorage revenue. The costs of higher inflation are borne by the rest of the society, most notably the reforming sector.

On the other hand, the trading interest in both sectors will push for stable exchange rates and monetary reintegration with the former Soviet republics or some peg to Western currencies, depending on the prevalent trading pattern. Those interests ultimately have a good chance to reestablish some currency arrangement. Thus again it could be shown that money ultimately follows trade, unless adverse circumstances shift the domestic political equilibrium.

The trading interests are also behind recent attempts of monetary integration in Western Europe. There is a second reason why the European states embarked on the idea of monetary union recently: Full capital mobility, an integral part of the common markets project of the European Union, renders fixed but adjustable exchange rates inherently unstable. The commitment to only fixed rates loses credibility with the markets and speculation can be destabilizing and rational, because self-fulfilling. Thus, minor shocks can cause speculation against the currencies' peg. By raising the exit costs of fixed exchange rates by full monetary union, it is hoped to reestablish the commitment of the countries' peg.

An important differentiation has to be made between large and small firms in the tradables sector. Small enterprises do not necessarily gain from monetary integration in Europe as the banking industry example proves. The example of the banking sector is interesting because it first pushes for full monetary union rather than only fixed exchange rates. Secondly, in contrast to the banking business in the nineteenth century, the banking industry this time supports monetary integration. The gains from monetary union overcompensate the losses from the reduced conversion business.

The last important interest group finally is bureaucracy and its influence on the collapse of the EMS. Public choice theory for long has held that bureaucrats have their own objectives as well, among which are maximizing independence and discretionary power. They will pursue those interests whenever possible. Monetary union negatively affects these interests of the German Bundesbank, one especially important actor in EMU. Fearing to lose its dominant role after the Maastricht Treaty, it used the opportunity provided by German unification to undermine the EMS countries' commitment to the European monetary arrangement.

8.2. The Desirability of Fixed Exchange Rates

Positive public choice studies usually close with the observation that the outcome of the political process is not optimal nor desirable. Therefore, normative public choice theory is concerned with the design of political institutions and mechanism that ensure that rent-seeking does not occur and that policymakers choose a better solution than when captured by interest groups. From this perspective, this study is different because I would argue that the desire of interest groups for fixed exchange rates is beneficial at least for the European economies.

This is so for several reasons: First, I believe that the benefits from monetary integration are often (deliberately) underestimated. This is due to the insufficient state of the economic theory regarding the role of money, as argued in the introduction. It often neglects the network externalities of money and thus fails to recognize an important factor.

Secondly, recent experiences suggest that exchange rates move excessively without being justified by "fundamental" factors. Foreign exchange markets might be inefficient and show features of destabilizing speculation. The real costs of these fluctuations could be avoided by restricting exchange rate fluctuations.

Third, this would be possible and less expensive than is usually maintained because the positive effects from exchange rate adaptation are overestimated. The notion that exchange rate adjustments can substitute for other necessary adjustments in the economy is less justified in an Europe where production structures become more and more alike. As Hayek argued already in 1937, the danger of creating distortions in other sectors of the economy by helping the one negatively affected through devaluation should be realized and taken into account.

Fourth, as recent developments in Europe show, the upheavals in the European monetary relations bear the danger of a movement to protectionist measures. Enterprises in the stable currency countries, like France and Germany, demand either the introduction of rapid monetary union or to levy compensatory tariffs on products from countries which devalue significantly. Exchange rate changes might thus be again the instrument of or the reason for protectionst measures. In the interwar years the collapse of trading blocs was accompanied by the collapse of currency relations as well, and states resorted to either exchange rate manipulation and/or tariff protection (see Simmons 1994). Monetary union would be one way to avoid a repetition of these experiences.

Fifth, monetary union would finally require that politicians recognize that the degrees of freedom in policymaking are restricted. As long as ultimate exchange rate alignments are the last way out, short-term considerations will give rise to inconsistent policies, such as the combination of monetary autonomy with fixed exchange rates. The promise of fixed rates is therefore time-inconsistent and markets know this. Speculation only hastens the collapse of inconsistent policies and arrangements.[3] Granting monetary autonomy to a single central bank in Europe is one way of solving this problem. The statutes of the European central bank are relatively save towards manipulation from policymakers (see Kenen 1992) and since political union is not very likely in the near future, opposing interests of nation states will avoid a common manipulation of all European economies.

This raises the question whether states will be willing to move towards full monetary union and thus to give up their ultimate instrument of money creation and exchange rate realignment. I would be optimistic because the balance of interests seems to tips towards monetary union in Europe. In other regions of the world, this solution is less probable and less desirable.

The three large currency blocs, the U.S., Japan and the EU, are not likely to give up policy autonomy among them. Economic structure is more diverse among them than among the EU countries and the political will for redistribution, which might be part of a currency union, is absent. For them domestic political considerations will be decisive. Given what was said above, this implies that currency relations among the blocs could become less stable under full capital mobility. This has also an implication for the international trading system. Exchange variability will trigger demands from those adversely affected to protect them against devaluations and thus tariffs, or other trade barriers, might be used to shelter domestic interests. Not only does trade require stable currency relations, but unstable currencies might also undermine the free trading system. This would then imply a world with several trading and currency blocs, relatively closed towards each other.

Notes

1. If asymmetric shocks in the tradables sector occurred, the same incentive would be given. But as argued, those shocks are increasingly unlikely. Moreover, the tradables sector faces two opposing effects. Even if output could be stabilized by money supply increases, the floating exchange rate would diminish that positive effect. Thus, I conclude that pressure to suspend the fixed rate is less likely to come from that sector.

2. The idea of a world coin unity is almost as old as the different monetary constitutions of countries (my translation).

3. This kind of speculation is different to the one referred to above. This speculation is not destabilizing but rooted in fundamentals. This is connected to the Krugman (1979) approach to balance-of-payments crises.

References

Alesina, Alberto. 1987. Macroeconomics and Politics in a Two-Party System as a Repeated Game, *Quarterly Journal of Economics* 102: 651-677.
_____, and Allan Drazen. 1991. Why Are Stabilizations Delayed?, *American Economic Review* 81:1170-1188.
_____, and Vittorio Grilli. 1993. On the Feasibility of a One-Speed or Multispeed European Monetary Union, *Economics and Politics* 5: 145-165.
Al-Marhubi, Fahim, and Thomas D. Willett. 1995. Determinants of Exchange Rate Regime Choice, Claremont Graduate School, unpublished manuscript.
Alogoskoufis, George, and Ron Smith. 1991. The Phillips-Curve, the Persistence of Inflation and the Lucas-Critique: Evidence from Exchange Rate Regimes, *American Economic Review* 81: 1254-1275.
Andersen, Torben, and Friedrich Schneider. 1986. Coordination of Fiscal and Monetary Policy Under Different Institutional Arrangements, *European Journal of Political Economy* 2: 169-191.
Axelrod, Robert. 1984. *The Evolution of Cooperation*, New York: Basic Books.
Baldwin, Richard E. 1991. On the Microeconomics of the European Monetary Union, *European Economy*, Special edition 1: 21-35.
_____, and Paul Krugman. 1989. Persistent Trade Effects of Large Exchange Rate Shocks, *Quarterly Journal of Economics* 104: 633-654.
Barro, Robert, and David Gordon. 1983. A Positive Theory of Monetary Policy in a Natural Rate Model, *Journal of Political Economy* 91: 589-610.
Bartel, Robert J. 1974. International Monetary Unions: The XIXth Century Experience, *Journal of European Economic History* 3: 689-704.
Baxter, Marianne, and Alan Stockman. 1989. Business Cycles and the Exchange Rate Regime: Some International Evidence, *Journal of Monetary Economics* 23: 377-400.
Bayoumi, Tamim. 1994. A Formal Model of Optimum Currency Areas, *IMF Staff Papers* 41: 537-554.
_____, and Barry Eichengreen. 1994. Macroeconomic Adjustment Under Bretton Woods and the Post-Bretton-Woods Float: An Impulse-Response Analysis, *Economic Journal* 104: 813-827.
Begg, David, and Charles Wyplosz. 1987. Why the EMS? Dynamic Games and the Equilibrium Policy Regime in: R. Bryant, and R. Portes, eds. *Global Macroeconomics*, London: Macmillan: 193-232.
Bensaid, Bernard, and Olivier Jeanne. 1994. The Instability of Fixed Exchange Rate System When Raising the Nominal Interest Rate is Costly, LSE Financial Markets Group Discussion Paper 190, July.
Bergman, Michael, Stefan Gerlach, and Lars Jonung. 1993. The Rise and Fall of the Scandinavian Currency Union 1873-1920, *European Economic Review* 37: 507-517.
Bernholz, Peter. 1982. Flexible Exchange Rates in Historical Perspective, Princeton Studies in International Finance 49.
_____. 1985. *The International Game of Power*, Berlin: Mouton.

_____. 1989. Currency Competition, Inflation, Gresham's Law and Exchange Rate, *Journal of Institutional and Theoretical Economics* 145: 465-488.

Bickel, Wilhelm. 1964. Die öffentlichen Finanzen, *Schweizerische Zeitschrift für Volkswirtschaft und Statistik* 100: 273-302.

Bini-Smaghi, Lorenzo, and Silvia Vori. 1992. Rating the EC as an Optimal Currency Area: Is it Worse than the US?, in R. O'Brien, ed: *Finance and the International Economy* 6, New York: Oxford University Press: 79-104.

Blanchard, Olivier J. 1990. Why Does Money Affect Output?: A Survey in B. Friedman, and F. Hahn, eds: *Handbook of Monetary Economics* II, Amsterdam: North-Holland: 779-835.

_____, and Lawrence F. Katz. 1992. Regional Evolutions, *Brookings Papers on Economic Activity*, No.1: 1-75.

_____, and Pierre-Alain Muet. 1993. Competitiveness through Disinflation: An Assessment of the French Macroeconomic Strategy, *Economic Policy* 16: 12-56.

Bloomfield, Arthur. 1959. *Monetary Policy Under the International Gold Standard, 1880-1914*, New York: Federal Reserve Bank of New York.

Bofinger, Peter. 1991a. Geld- und Kreditpolitik nach Bildung der deutschen Währungsunion, in H. Gröner, E. Kantzenbach, and O. Meyer, eds: *Wirtschaftspolitische Probleme der Integration der ehemaligen DDR in die Bundesrepublik*, Berlin: Duncker&Humblot: 151-175.

_____. 1991b. Options for the Payment Systems and Exchange-Rate System in Eastern Europe, *European Economy* Special Edition 2: 243-262.

_____. 1994. Is Europe an Optimum Currency Area?, CEPR discussion paper 915, February.

_____, Eirik Svindland, and Benedikt Thanner. 1993. Prospects of the Monetary Order in Republics of the FSU, in *The Economics of New Currencies*, London: Centre for Economic Policy Research: 9-33.

Borchardt, Knut. 1985. Die industrielle Revolution in Deutschland 1750-1914, in : C. Cipolla, and K. Borchardt, eds: *Europäische Wirtschaftsgeschichte* Vol. 4, Stuttgart: Gustav Fischer: 135-202.

Bordo, Michael D., and Finn E. Kydland. 1995. The Gold Standard as a Rule, *Explorations in Economic History* 32: 423-464.

BVR. Bundesverband der deutschen Volksbanken und Raiffeisenbanken., *Annual Report*, various issues.

Bundesbank. 1991. *Monthly Report October*, Frankfurt.

_____. *Auszüge aus Presseartikeln*, various issues.

Cafagna, Luciano. 1985. Die industrielle Revolution in Italien 1830-1914, in C. Cipolla, and K. Borchardt, eds: *Europäische Wirtschaftsgeschichte* 4, Stuttgart: Fischer: 63-84.

Canals, Jordi. 1993. *Competitive Strategies in European Banking*, Oxford: Clarendon Press.

Canzoneri, Matthew B. 1985. Monetary Policy Games and the Role of Private Information, *American Economic Review* 75: 1056-1070.

_____, and Jo Anna Gray. 1983. Two Essays on Monetary Policy in an Interdependent World, International Finance Discussion Paper 219, Federal Reserve Board.

_____, and Carol Ann Rogers. 1990. Is the European Community an Optimum Currency Area? Optimal Taxation versus the Costs of Multiple Currencies, *American Economic Review* 80: 419-433.

Casella, Alessandra. 1992a. On Markets and Clubs: Economic and Political Integration of Regions with Unequal Productivity, *American Economic Review* Papers and Proceedings 82: 115-121.

_____. 1992b. Participation in a Currency Union, *American Economic Review* 2: 847-863.

_____, and Barry Eichengreen. 1996. Can Foreign Aid Accelerate Stabilization?, *Economic Journal* 103:605-619.

_____, and Jonathan Feinstein. 1989. Management of a Common Currency, in M. De Cecco, and A. Giovannini, eds: *A European Central Bank?*, Cambridge: Cambridge University Press: 131-155.

Cassing, James, Timothy McKeown, and Jack Ochs. 1986. The Political Economy of the Tariff Cycle, *American Political Science Review* 80: 843-862.

Christensen, Benedicte Vibe. 1994. The Russian Federation in Transition, IMF Occasional paper 111, February.

Clough, Shepard B. 1964. *The Economic History of Modern Italy*, New York: Columbia University Press.

Cohen, Benjamin J. 1989. European Financial Integration and National Banking Interests, in P. Guerrieri, and P. C. Padoan, eds: *The Political Economy of European Integration*, New York: Harvester-Wheastsheaf: 145-170.

_____. 1993. Beyond EMU: The Problem of Sustainability, *Economics and Politics* 5: 187-203.

Cohen, Daniel, and Charles Wyplosz. 1989. The European Monetary Union: An Agnostic Evaluation, in: R. Bryant et al, eds: *Macroeconomic Policy in an Interdependent World*, Washington: Brookings: 311-342.

Collins, Susan, and Francesco Giavazzi. 1993. Attitudes Towards Inflation and the Variability of Fixed Exchange Rates, in: M. Bordo, and B. Eichengreen, eds: *A Retrospective on the Bretton Woods System*, Chicago: University of Chicago Press: 547-577.

Cooper, Richard N. 1985. Economic Interdependence and Coordination of Economic Policies, in R. W. Jones, and P. B. Kenen, eds: *Handbook of International Economics* II, Amsterdam: Elsevier: 1195-1234.

Corden, W. Max. 1972. Monetary Integration, Princeton Essays in International Finance 93.

_____. 1982. Exchange Rate Protection in: R. N. Cooper, P. B. Kenen, J. B. de Macedo, J. van Ypersele, eds: *The International Monetary System under Flexible Exchange Rates*, Cambridge: Ballinger: 17-33.

_____. 1993. European Monetary Union: The Intellectual Pre-History in: *The Monetary Future of Europe*, London: Centre for Economic Policy Research.

_____. 1994. *Economic Policy, Exchange Rates and the International System*, Chicago: Chicago University Press.

De Cecco, Marcello. 1992. European Monetary and Financial Cooperation Before the First World War, *Rivista di Storia Economica* 9: 55-76.

146   References

De Grauwe, Paul. 1993. The Political Economy of Monetary Union in Europe, *World Economy* 16: 653-661.

_____. 1994. *The Economics of Monetary Integration*, Oxford: Oxford University Press, 2nd edition.

_____, and Bernard de Bellefroid. 1989. Long-Run Exchange Rate Variability and International Trade, in S. Arndt, and D. Richardson, eds: *Real Financial Linkages Among Open Economies*, Cambridge: MIT-Press: 193-212.

De Kock, Gabriel, and Vittorio Grilli. 1993. Fiscal Policies and the Choice of Exchange Rate Regime, *Economic Journal* 103: 347-358.

Dewatripont, Mathias, and Gérard Roland. 1992. The Virtues of Gradualism and Legitimacy in the Transition to a Market Economy, *Economic Journal* 102: 291-300.

Dixit, Avinash. 1989. Hysteresis, Imports Penetration, and Exchange Rate Pass-Through, *Quarterly Journal of Economics* 104: 205-227.

Dornbusch, Rudiger. 1992. Monetary Problems of Post-Communism: Lessons from the End of the Austro-Hungarian Empire, *Weltwirtschaftliches Archiv* 128: 391-424.

_____, Federico Sturzenegger, and Holger Wolf. 1990. Extreme Inflations: Dynamics and Stabilization, *Brookings Papers on Economic Activity* 2: 1-84.

Dowd, Kevin, and David Greenaway. 1993. Currency Competition, Network Externalities and Switching Costs: Towards an Alternative View of Optimum Currency Areas, *Economic Journal 103*: 1180-1189.

Drazen, Allan, and Vittorio Grilli. 1993. The Benefit of Crisis for Economic Reform, *American Economic Review* 83: 598-607.

_____, and Paul R. Masson. 1994. Credibility of Policies vs. Credibility of Policy-makers, *Quarterly Journal of Economics* 109: 735-754.

Dubois, Louis-Albert. 1950. *La Fin de l'Union Monétaire Latine*, Arbois: Jules Guinchard.

Edwards, Sebastian. 1993. Exchange Rates as Nominal Anchors, *Weltwirtschaftliches Archiv* 129: 1-32.

Eichengreen, Barry. 1992. *Golden Fetters: The Gold Standard and the Great Depression 1919-1939*, New York: Oxford University Press.

_____. 1993a. European Monetary Integration, *Journal of Economic Literature* 31: 1321-1357.

_____. 1993b. A Payments Mechanism for the Former Soviet Union: Is the EPU a Revelant Precedent?, *Economic Policy* 17: 310-353.

_____. 1993c. The Crisis in the EMS and the Transition to EMU: An Interim Assessment, University of California at Berkeley, unpublished manuscript.

_____. 1995. *A History of the International Monetary System*, University of California at Berkeley, unpublished manuscript.

_____, and Marc Flandreau. 1994. The Geography of the Gold Standard, CEPR discussion paper 1050, October.

_____, and Jeffry Frieden. 1993. The Political Economy of European Monetary Unification: An Analytical Introduction, *Economics and Politics* 5: 85-104.

_____, and Fabio Ghironi. 1995. European Monetary Unification: The Challenges Ahead, in F. Torres, ed: *Monetary Reform in Europe*, Lisbon: Universidade Católica Editora: 83-120.

_____, and Charles Wyplosz. 1993. The Unstable EMS, *Brookings Papers on Economic Activity* 1: 51-143.

Epstein, Gerald. 1991. Profit Squeeze, Rentier Squeeze and Macroeconomic Policy Under Fixed and Flexible Exchange Rates, *Economies et Sociétés* 25.3: 219-257.

Esslen, Joseph Bergfried. 1917. Vergangenheit und Zukunft des Lateinischen Münzbundes, *Bank Archiv* 16: 125-132 and 150-158.

Ethier, Wilfried. 1973. International Trade and the Forward Exchange Market, *American Economic Review* 63: 494-503.

_____. 1992. International Trade and Payments Mechanisms: Options and Possibilities, Another View, in A. Hillman, and B. Milanovic, eds: *The Transition form Socialism in Eastern Europe*, Washington: The World Bank: 313-328.

European Commission. 1990. *One Market, One Money*, European Economy 44, October.

Fischer, Wolfram. 1960. The German Zollverein, *Kyklos* 13: 65-89.

Flandreau, Marc. 1993a. On the Inflationary Bias of Common Currencies: The Latin Union Puzzle, *European Economic Review* 37: 501-506.

_____. 1993b. Trade, Finance and Currency Blocs in 19th Century Europe: Was the Latin Monetary Union a Franc-Zone?, University of California at Berkeley, unpublished manuscript.

Flood, Robert P., and Peter M. Garber. 1984. Gold Monetization and Gold Discipline, *Journal of Political Economy* 92: 90-107.

_____, and Michael Mussa. 1994. Issues Concerning Nominal Anchors for Monetary Policy in T. Baliño, and C. Cottarelli, eds: *Frameworks for Monetary Stability*, Washington: IMF: 42-77.

Frankel, Jeffrey A., and Shang-Jin Wei. 1993. Emerging Currency Blocs, University of California at Berkeley, unpublished manuscript.

Franz, Wolfgang; Gustav Heidbrink, and Werner Smolny. 1993. The Impact of German Unification of West Germany's Goods and Labor Market: A Macroeconomic Disequlibrium Model in Action, University of Konstanz, unpublished manuscript.

Fratianni, Michele, and Franco Spinelli. 1985. Currency Competition, Fiscal Policy and the Money Supply Process in Italy from Unification to World War I, *Journal of European Economic History* 14: 473-499.

_____, and Jürgen von Hagen. 1992. *The European Monetary System and European Monetary Union*, Boulder: Westview.

Frey, Bruno S., and Friedrich Schneider. 1981. Central Bank Behavior: A Positive Empirical Analysis, *Journal of Monetary Economics* 7: 291-315.

Frieden, Jeffry. 1991. Invested Interests: The Politics of National Economic Policys in a World of Global Finance, *International Organization* 45: 425-451.

_____. 1994. Exchange Rate Politics: Contemporary Lessons from American History, *Review of International Political Economy* 1: 81-103.

Friedman, Milton. 1953. The Case for Flexible Exchange Rates in M. Friedman: *Essays in Positive Economics*, Chicago: University of Chicago Press: 157-203.

_____.1990. Bimetallism Revisted, *Journal of Economic Perspectives* 4: 85-104.

Gärtner, Manfred, and Heinrich W. Ursprung. 1989. Politische und Ökonomische Gesetze für Flexible Wechselkurse, *Jahrbuch für Neue Politische Ökonomie* 8: 109-125.

Gallarotti, Giulio. 1985. Toward a Business-Cycle Model of Tariffs, *International Organization* 39: 155-187.

———. 1993. The Scramble for Gold: Monetary Regime Transformation in the 1870s, in M. Bordo, and F. Capie, eds: *Monetary Regimes in Transition*, Cambridge: Cambridge University Press: 15-67.

Garber, Peter M., and Michael G. Spencer. 1994. The Dissolution of the Austro-Hungarian Empire: Lessons for Currency Reform, Princeton Essays in International Finance 191.

———, and Mark P. Taylor. 1995. Sand in the Wheels of Foreign Exchange Markets: A Sceptical Note, *Economic Journal* 105: 173-180.

Garrett, Geoffrey. 1993. The Politics of Maastricht, *Economics and Politics* 5: 105-123.

Gerschenkron, Alexander. 1943. *Bread and Democracy in Germany*, Berkeley: University of California Press.

Giavazzi, Francesco, and Alberto Giovannini. 1989. *Limiting Exchange Flexibility*, Cambridge: MIT-Press.

———, and Marco Pagano. 1988. The Advantage of Tying One's Hands: EMS Discipline and Central Bank Credibility, *European Economic Review* 32: 1055-1082.

Giovannini, Alberto. 1989. How Do Fixed Exchange Rate Regimes Work? Evidence From the Gold Standard, Bretton Woods and the EMS in: M. Miller, R. Portes, and B. Eichengreen, eds: *Blueprints for Exchange Rate Management*, New York: Academic Press: 13-41.

———. 1993a. Bretton Woods and its Precursors: Rules Versus Discretion in the History of International Monetary Regimes, in M. Bordo, and B. Eichengreen, eds: *A Retrospective on the Bretton Woods System*, Chicago: Chicago University Press: 109-147.

———. 1993b. Central Banking in a Monetary Union: Reflections on the Proposed Statute of the European Central Bank, *Carnegie-Rochester Conference Series on Public Policy* 38: 191-230.

———. 1993c. Economic and Monetary Union: What Happened?--Exploring the Political Dimension of Optimum Currency Areas, in: *The Monetary Future of Europe*, London: Centre for Economic Policy Research.

Goldberg, Linda S., Barry W. Ickes, and Randi Ryterman. 1994. Departure From the Ruble Zone: The Implications of Adopting Independent Currencies, *World Economy* 17: 293-322.

Goodhart, Charles. 1988. *The Evolution of Central Banks*, Cambridge: MIT-Press.

Goodman, John B. 1992. *Monetary Sovereignty: The Politics of Central Banking in Western Europe*, Ithaca: Cornell University Press.

Gourevitch, Peter Alexis. 1977. International Trade, Domestic Coalitions, and Liberty: The Crisis of 1873-1896, *Journal of Interdisciplinary History* 8: 281-313.

Grilli, Vittorio. 1989. Exchange Rates and Seigniorage, *European Economic Review* 33: 580-587.

Gros, Daniel. 1992. Capital Controls and Foreign Exchange Market Crises in the EMS, *European Economic Review* 36: 1533-1544.

———, and Alfred Steinherr. 1995. *Winds of Change: Economic Transition in Central and Eastern Europe*, London: Longman.

_____, and Niels Thygesen. 1992. *European Monetary Integration*, London: Longman.

Grüner, Hans Peter, and Carsten Hefeker. 1995. Domestic Pressures and the Exchange Rate Regime: Why Economically Bad Decisions are Politically Popular, *Banca Nazionale del Lavoro Quarterly Review* 194: 331-350.

_____, and _____ 1996. Bank Cooperation and Banking Policy in a Monetary Union: A Political-Economy Perspective on EMU, *Open Economies Review* 7: 183-198.

Haggard, Stephan, and Beth A. Simmons. 1987. Theories of International Regimes, *International Organization* 41: 491-517.

Hartwig, Karl-Hans. 1984. Bundesbankautonomie und Inflationsbekämpfung: Politische Ökonomie des Notenbankverhaltens, *List-Forum* 12: 307-322.

Havrilesky, Thomas. 1994. The Political Economy of Monetary Policy, *European Journal of Political Economy* 10: 111-134.

Havrylyshyn, Oleh. 1994. Reviving Trade Amongst the Newly Independent States, *Economic Policy* 19. Supplement.: 172-190.

_____, and John Williamson. 1991. *From Soviet disUnion to Eastern Economic Community?*, Washington: Institute for International Economics.

Hayek, Friedrich A. 1937. *Monetary Nationalism and International Stability*, London: Longmans Green (New York: Augustus Kelley, reprint 1989.

Hefeker, Carsten. 1994. German Monetary Union, the Bundesbank and the EMS Collapse, *Banca Nazionale del Lavoro Quarterly Review* 191: 379-398.

_____. 1995a. Monetary Union or Currency Competition? Currency Arrangements for Monetary Stability in East and West, *Constitutional Political Economy* 6: 57-69.

_____. 1995b. Interest Groups, Coalitions and Monetary Integration in the 19th Century, *Journal of European Economic History* 24: 489-536.

_____. 1996a. The Political Choice and Collapse of Fixed Exchange Rates, *Journal of Institutional and Theoretical Economics* 152: 360-379.

_____. 1996b. Germany and European Monetary Union, in J. Frieden, D. Gros, and E. Jones, eds: *Towards European Monetary Union: Problems and Prospects*, forthcoming.

_____. 1996c. Distributional Conflict, Trade and Monetary Nationalism in the Former Soviet Union, Centre for European Policy Studies, unpublished manuscript.

Helfferich, Karl. 1894. *Die Folgen des Deutsch-Österreichischen Münz-Vereins von 1857*, Straßburg.

_____. 1895. Die geschichtliche Entwicklung der Münzsysteme, *Jahrbücher für Nationalökonomie und Statistik* 9: 801-828.

_____. 1923. *Das Geld*, Leipzig.

Henderson, William O. 1968. *The Zollverein*, London: Frank Cass, 2nd edition.

Henning, C. Randall. 1994. *Currencies and Politics in the United States, Germany and Japan*, Washington: Institute for International Economics.

Hibbs, Douglas A. 1977. Political Parties and Macroeconomic Policy, *American Political Science Review* 71: 1467-1487.

Hillman, Arye L. 1989. *The Political Economy of Protection*, Chur: Harwood.

_____. 1994. The Transition from Socialism: An Overview from a Political Economy Perspective, *European Journal of Political Economy* 10: 191-225.

_____, Manuel Hinds, Branko Milanovic, and Heinrich Ursprung. 1993. Protectionist Pressures and Enterprise Restructuring: The Political Economy of International Trade Policy in the Transition, The World Bank, unpublished manuscript.

Holtfrerich, Carl-Ludwig. 1989. The Monetary Unification Process in 19th Century Germany: Relevance and Lessons for Europe Today, in: M. De Cecco, and A. Giovannini, eds: *A European Central Bank?*, Cambridge: Cambridge University Press: 216-242.

_____. 1993. Did Monetary Unification Preceede or Follow Political Unification of Germany in the 19th Century, *European Economic Review* 37: 518-524.

Honkapohja, Seppo, and Pentti Pikkarainen. 1994. Country Characteristics and the Choice of the Exchange Rate Regime: Are Mini-Shirts are Followed by Maxis?, in J. Åkerholm, and A. Giovannini, eds: *Exchange Rate Policy in the Nordic Countries*, Cambridge: Cambridge University Press: 31-53.

Horn, Henrik, and Torsten Persson. 1988. Exchange Rate Policy, Wage Formation and Credibility, *European Economic Review* 32: 1621-1636.

Hughes Hallett, Andrew, and Yue Ma. 1993. East Germany, West Germany, and their Mezzogiorno Problem: A Parable for European Economic Integration, *Economic Journal* 103: 416-428.

Irwin, Douglas A. 1993. Multilateral and Bilateral Trade Policies in the World Trading System: An Historical Perspective, in J. de Melo, and A. Panagariya, eds: *New Dimensions in Regional Integration*, Cambridge: Cambridge University Press: 90-119.

Ishiyama, Yoshihide. 1975. The Theory of Optimum Curreny Areas: A Survey, *IMF Staff Papers* 22: 344-383.

James, Harold. 1995. The IMF and the Creation of the Bretton Woods System, 1944-58, in B. Eichengreen, ed: *Europe's Post-War Recovery*, Cambridge: Cambridge University Press: 93-126.

Janssen, Albert E. 1911. *Les Conventions Monétaires*, Paris: Alcan&Lisbonne.

Kenen, Peter B. 1969. The Theory of Optimum Currency Areas: An Eclectic View, in R. Mundell, and A. Swoboda, eds: *Monetary Problems of the International Economy*, Chicago: University of Chicago Press: 41-60.

_____. 1991. Transitional Arrangements for Trade and Payments among the CMEA Countries, *IMF Staff Papers* 38: 235-267.

_____. 1992. *EMU After Maastricht*, Washington: Group of Thirty.

_____. 1994. Floating Exchange Rates Reconsidered: The Influence of New Ideas, Priorities and Problems, in P. Kenen, F. Papadia, and F. Saccomani, eds: *The International Monetary System*, Cambridge: Cambridge University Press: 139-161.

_____. 1995a. Capital Controls, the EMS and EMU, *Economic Journal* 105: 181-192.

_____. 1995b. *Economic and Monetary Union in Europe. Moving Beyond Maastricht*, Cambridge: Cambridge University Press.

Keohane, Robert O. 1984. *After Hegemony--Cooperation and Discord in the World Political Economy*, New Jersey: Princeton University Press.

Keynes, John Maynard. 1923. *A Tract on Monetary Reform*, reprinted as Vol IV of the Collected Writings of Keynes, London: Macmillan St. Martin's Press, 1971.

Kindleberger, Charles P. 1975. The Rise of Free Trade in Western Europe, *Journal of Economic History* 35: 20-55.

_____. 1986. International Public Goods Without Government, *American Economic Review* 76, 1-13.

Kiyotaki, Nobuhiro, and Randall Wright. 1989. On Money as a Medium of Exchange, *Journal of Political Economy* 97: 827-854.

Krämer, Hans R. 1971. Experiences with Historical Monetary Unions, in H. Giersch, ed: *Integration durch Währungsunion?*, Tübingen: Mohr: 106-118.

Kröger, Jürgen, and Manfred Teutemann. 1992. The German Economy After Unification: Domestic and European Aspects, *Economic Papers* 91, Commission of the European Community.

Kronman, Anthony T. 1985. Contract Law and the State of Nature, *Journal of Law, Economics and Organization* 1: 5-32.

Krugman, Paul. 1979. A Model of Balance-of-Payments Crises, *Journal of Money, Credit and Banking* 11: 311-325.

_____. 1989. The Case for Stabilizing Exchange Rates, *Oxford Review of Economic Policy* 5: 61-72.

_____. 1991. *Geography and Trade*, Cambridge: MIT-Press.

_____. 1993. What Do We Need to Know about the International Monetary System?, Princeton Essays in International Finance 190.

Kydland, Finn E., and Edward Prescott. 1977. Rules Rather than Discretion: The Inconsistency of Optimal Plans, *Journal of Political Economy* 85: 473-491.

Laban, Raul, and Federico Sturzenegger. 1994. Distributional Conflicts, Financial Adaptation and Delayed Stabilization, *Economics and Politics* 6: 257-276.

Lambi, Ivo Nicolai. 1963. *Free Trade and Protection in Germany 1868-1879*, Wiesbaden: Steiner.

Lazaretou, Sophia. 1995. Government Spending, Monetary Policies, and Exchange Rate Regime Switches: The Drachma in the Gold Standard Period, *Explorations in Economic History* 32: 28-50.

Lipp, Ernst-Moritz, Ulrich Ramm, and Norbert Walter. 1992. Stellungnahme zum Manifest der über 60 Profesoren über die Maastricht-Beschlüsse zur Europäischen Wirtschafts-und Währungsunion, in *Auszüge aus Presseartikeln*, Deutsche Bundesbank, June 16: 1-2.

Lipton, David, and Jeffrey D. Sachs. 1992. Prospects for Russia's Reforms, *Brookings Papers on Economic Activity* 2: 213-283.

Lohmann, Susanne. 1993a. Electoral Cycles and International Policy Coordination, *European Economic Review* 37: 1373-1391.

_____. 1993b. Political Business Cycles in a Federal System: West Germany, 1960-1989, Stanford University, unpublished manuscript.

Mac Rae, C. Duncan. 1977. A Political Model of the Business Cycle, *Journal of Political Economy* 85: 239-263.

Magnifico, Giovanni. 1973. *European Monetary Integration*, London: Macmillan.

Marsh, David. 1992. *The Bank That Rules Europe*, London: Heinemann.

Masson, Paul R., and Mark P. Taylor. 1993. Currency Unions: A Survey of the Issues in: P. Masson, and M. Taylor, eds: *Policy Issues in the Operation of Currency Unions*, Cambridge: Cambridge University Press: 3-51.

Matsuyama, Kiminori, Nobuhiro Kiyotaki, and Akihiko Matsui. 1993. Toward a Theory of International Currency, *Review of Economic Studies* 60: 283-307.

Mc Culloch, Rachel. 1983. Unexpected Real Consequences of Floating Exchange Rates, Princeton Essays in International Finance 153.

Mc Keown, Timothy. 1983. Hegemonic Stability Theories and the 19th-Century Tariff Levels in Europe, *International Organization* 37: 73-91.

Mc Kinnon, Ronald. 1963. Optimum Currency Areas, *American Economic Review* 53: 717-725.

————. 1991. Stabilizing the Ruble: The Problem of Internal Currency Convertibility in E.-M. Claassen, ed: *Exchange Rate Policies in Developing and Post-Socialist Countries*, San Francisco: ICS Press: 59-87.

Melitz, Jacques. 1988. Monetary Discipline and Cooperation in the European Monetary System: A Synthesis, in F. Giavazzi, S. Micossi, and M. Miller, eds: *The European Monetary System*, Cambridge: Cambridge University Press: 51-78.

————. 1991. German Reunification and Exchange Rate Policy in the EMS, CEPR discussion paper 520, February.

————. 1993. The Theory of Optimum Currency Areas, Trade Adjustment and Trade, CEPR discussion paper 847, October.

Michalopoulos, Constantine, and David G. Tarr. 1994. Summary and Overview of Developments Since Independence in C. Michalopoulos, and D. Tarr, eds: *Trade in the New Independent States*, Washington: The World Bank: 1-21.

Milesi-Feretti, Gian Maria. 1995a. The Dynamics of Inflation and Capital Accumulation in Previously Centrally Planned Economies: A Theoretical Framework, *Economica* 62: 441-459.

————. 1995b. The Disadvantage of Tying Their Hands: On the Political Economy of Policy Commitments, *Economic Journal* 105: 1381-1402.

Miller, Marcus H. 1993. The Break-up of the Ruble Zone and Prospects for a New Ukranian Currency: A Monetary Analysis, in *The Economics of New Currencies*, London: Centre for Economic Policy Research: 113-136.

Mundell, Robert. 1961. A Theory of Optimum Currency Areas, *American Economic Review* 51: 657-665.

Mussa, Michael. 1990. Exchange Rates in Theory and Reality, Princeton Essays in International Finance 179.

Neumann, Manfred J. M. 1992. German Unification: Economic Problems and Consequences, *Carnegie-Rochester Conference Series on Public Policy* 36: 163-209.

Nordhaus, William D. 1975. The Political Business Cycle, *Review of Economic Studies* 42: 169-190.

Nurkse, Ragnar. 1944. *International Currency Experience*, Geneva: League of Nations.

Obstfeld, Maurice. 1986. Rational and Self-Fulfilling Balance of Payments Crises, *American Economic Review* 76: 72-81.

————. 1994. The Logic of Currency Crises, NBER discussion paper 4640, February.

————, and Kenneth Rogoff. 1995. The Mirage of Fixed Exchange Rates, *Journal of Economic Perspectives* 9. Fall: 73-96.

Olson, Mancur. 1965. *The Logic of Collective Action*, Cambridge: Harvard University Press.

Ozkan, F. Gulcin, and Alan Sutherland. 1994. A Model of the ERM Crises, CEPR discussion paper 879, January.

_____, and _____. 1995. Policy Measures to Avoid Currency Crisis, *Economic Journal* 105: 510-519.

Peltzman, Sam. 1976. Toward a More General Theory of Regulation, *Journal of Law and Economics* 19: 211-248.

Perée, Eric, and Alfred Steinherr. 1989. Exchange Rate Uncertainty and Foreign Trade, *European Economic Review* 33: 1241-1264.

Persson, Torsten, and Guido Tabellini. 1990. *Macroeconomic Policy, Credibility and Politics*, Chur: Harwood.

Pollard, Sidney. 1981. *The Integration of the European Economy Since 1815*, London: Allen&Unwin.

Portes, Richard. 1993. EMS and EMU After the Fall, *The World Economy* 16: 1-15.

Potters, Jan, and Frans van Winden. 1994. Models of Interest Groups. Four Different Approaches, CREED and University of Amsterdam, unpublished manuscript.

Redish, Angela. 1993a. The Latin Monetary Union and the Emergence of the International Gold Standard, in M. Bordo, and F. Capie, eds: *Monetary Regimes in Transition*, Cambridge: Cambridge University Press: 68-85.

_____. 1993b. Anchors Aweigh: The Transition from Commodity Money to Fiat Money in Western Economies, *Canadian Journal of Economics* 26: 777-795.

Rogoff, Kenneth. 1985a. Can International Policy Coordination be Counterproductive? *Journal of International Economics* 18: 199-217.

_____. 1985b. The Optimal Degree of Commitment to an Intermediate Monetary Target, *Quarterly Journal of Economics* 100: 1169-1189.

_____. 1990. Equilibrium Budget Cycles, *American Economic Review* 80: 21-36.

_____, and Anne Sibert. 1988. Elections and Macroeconomic Policy, *Review of Economic Studies* 55: 1-16.

Rogowski, Ronald. 1989. *Commerce and Coalition*, Princeton: Princeton University Press.

Rolnick, Arthur J., Bruce D. Smith, and Warren E. Weber. 1994. The Origins of the Monetary Union in the United States, in P. Siklos, ed: *Varities of Monetary Reforms*, Boston: Kluwer: 323-349.

_____, and Warren E. Weber. 1986. Greshams's Law or Gresham's Fallacy?, *Journal of Political Economy* 94: 185-199.

Romer, David. 1993. Openness and Inflation: Theory and Evidence, *Quarterly Journal of Economics* 108: 869-903.

Ruland, L.J., and J.-M. Viaene. 1993. The Political Choice of Exchange Rate Regimes, *Economics and Politics* 5: 271-284.

Sala-i-Martin, Xavier, and Jeffrey Sachs. 1992. Fiscal Federalism and Optimum Currency Areas: Evidence for Europe from the United States, in M. Canzoneri, V. Grilli, and P. Masson, eds. *Establishing a Central Bank*, Cambridge: Cambridge University Press: 195-219.

Sandholtz, Wayne. 1993. Choosing Union: Monetary Politics and Maastricht, *International Organization* 47: 1-39.

Sanucci, Valeria. 1989. The Establishment of a Central Bank: Italy in the 19th Century, in: M. De Cecco, and A. Giovannini, eds: *A European Central Bank?*, Cambridge: Cambridge University Press: 244-290.

Sargent, Thomas, and Francois Velde. 1990. The Analytics of German Monetary Unification, *Federal Reserve Bank of San Francisco Economic Review:* 33-51

Savvides, Andreas. 1990. Real Exchange Rate Variability and the Choice of Exchange Rate Regime By Developing Countries, *Journal of International Money and Finance* 9: 440-454.

Schuknecht, Ludger. 1992. *Trade Protection in the European Community*, Chur: Harwood.

Siebert, Horst. 1991. German Unification: The Economics of Transition, *Economic Policy* 13: 287-340.

Simmons, Beth. 1994. *Who Adjusts? Domestic Sources of Foreign Economic Policy During the Interwar Years*, Princeton: Princeton University Press.

Snidal, Duncan. 1985. The Limits to Hegemonic Stability Theory, *International Organization* 39: 579-614.

Stephan, Joerg. 1994. *A Political-Economic Analysis of Exchange Rate Movements*, Konstanz: Hartung und Gorre.

Stigler, George J. 1971. The Theory of Regulation, *Bell Journal of Economics and Management Science* 2: 3-21.

Svensson, Lars E.O. 1994. Fixed Exchange Rates as a Means to Price Stability: What have We Learned?, *European Economic Review* 38: 447-468.

Tavlas, George S. 1993. The 'New' Theory of Optimum Currency Areas, *World Economy* 16: 663-685.

Temin, Peter. 1989. *Lessons from the Great Depression*, Cambridge: MIT-Press.

Theurl, Theresia. 1992. *Eine gemeinsame Währung für Europa--12 Lehren aus der Geschichte*, Innsbruck: Österreichischer Studienverlag.

Tower, Edward, and Thomas D. Willett. 1976. The Theory of Optimum Currency Areas and Exchange Rate Flexibility, Princeton Special Papers in International Economics 11.

Triffin, Robert. 1947. National Central Banking and the International Economy, *Postwar Economic Studies* 7: 46-81.

Trimborn, Wilhelm. 1931. *Der Weltwährungsgedanke*, Jena: G. Fischer.

Ursprung, Heinrich W. 1991. Economic Policies and Political Competition in: A. L. Hillman, ed: *Markets and Politicians*, Dordrecht: Kluwer: 1-25.

van der Ploeg, Frederick. 1989. The Political Economy of Overvaluation, *Economic Journal* 99: 850-855.

Vaubel, Roland. 1980. The Return to the New EMS: Objectives, Incentives, Perspectives, *Carnegie-Rochester Conference Series on Public Policy* 13: 173-221.

_____. 1990. Currency Competition and European Monetary Integration, *Economic Journal* 100: 930-940.

_____. 1991. A Public Choice View of the Delors Report, in: R. Vaubel, and T. Willett, eds: *The Political Economy of International Organization*, Boulder: Westview: 306-310.

_____. 1993. Eine Public-Choice Analyse der Deutschen Bundesbank und ihre Implikationen für die Europäische Währungsunion in D. Duwendag, and J. Siebke, eds: *Europa vor dem Eintritt in die Wirtschafts- und Währungsunion*, Berlin: Duncker&Humblodt: 23-79.

_____. 1994. The Breakdown of the ERM and the Future of EMU: Explanations, Predictions and Simulations from a Public Choice Perspective, in D. Cobham, ed: *European Monetary Upheavals*, Manchester: Manchester University Press: 32-58.

Veit, Otto. 1969. *Grundriß der Währungspolitik*, Frankfurt/M.: Knapp, 3rd ed.

Viñals, José. 1996. European Monetary Integration: A Narrow Or a Wider EMU?, *European Economic Review* 40, 1103-1109.

Viner, Jacob. 1932. International Aspects of the Gold Standard in: Q. Wright, ed: *Gold and Monetary Stabilization*, Chicago: University of Chicago Press: 3-39.

_____. 1950. *The Customs Union Issue*, New York: Carnegie Endowment for International Peace.

Vives, Xavier. 1991. Banking Competition and European Integration in A. Giovannini, and C. Mayer, eds: *European Financial Integration*, Cambridge: Cambridge University Press: 9-31.

Von Hagen, Jürgen. 1992. German Unification: Economic Problems and Consequences. A Comment, *Carnegie-Rochester Conference Series on Public Policy* 36: 211-222.

Weber, Ernst-Juerg. 1988. Currency Competition in Switzerland 1826-1850, *Kyklos* 41: 459-478.

Weber, Manfred. 1993. Die Europäische Währungsunion aus Sicht der deutschen Banken, manuscript, October.

Weingast, Barry R., and William J. Marshall. 1988. The Industrial Organization of Congress or, Why Legislatures, Like Firms, are not Organized as Markets, *Journal of Political Economy* 96: 132-163.

Wihlborg, Clas, and Thomas D. Willett. 1991. Optimum Currency Areas Revisited on the Transition Path to a Currency Union in C. Wihlborg, M. Fratianni, and T. Willett, eds: *Financial Regulation and Monetary Arrangements after 1992*, Amsterdam: Elsevier: 279-297.

Willett, Thomas D., ed. 1988. *Political Business Cycles*, Durham: Duke University Press.

_____. 1996. The Public Choice Approach to International Economic Relations, Claremont Graduate School, unpublished manuscript.

_____, and Fahim Al-Marhubi. 1994. Inflation Control in the Formerly Centrally Planned Economies, *The World Economy* 17: 795-815.

Williamson, John. 1992. *Trade and Payments after Soviet Dissolution*, Washington: Institute for International Economics.

Willis, Henry Parker. 1901. *A History of the Latin Monetary Union*, Chicago: Chicago University Press (reprint New York: Greenwood Press, 1968).

Wyplosz, Charles. 1986. Capital Controls and Balance of Payments Crises, *Journal of International Money and Finance* 5: 167-179.

_____. 1991. On the Real Exchange Rate Effects of German Unification, *Weltwirtschaftliches Archiv* 127: 1-17.

Index

About the Book and Author

This book analyzes monetary integration and the choice and collapse of exchange rate regimes from a positive political economy perspective. Carsten Hefeker's approach offers new insights to the widely discussed, but only incompletely understood, topic of exchange rate regime choice. A coherent framework is developed, which challenges the traditional and normative theory of monetary integration by focusing on interest groups such as industries and bureaucracies to analyze how they influence policymakers and the outcome of economic policy. Hefeker shows that European monetary integration in the last century and today, as well as monetary disintegration in the former Soviet Union, can be interpreted and understood in this perspective.

Carsten Hefeker is a faculty member of the Department of Economics at the University of Basel.